OPERATION GRIZZLY BEAR

LANCE CRAIGHEAD

John and Frank Craighead taking an immobilized grizzly bear from a culvert trap in Yellowstone National Park

Operation GRIZZLY BEAR

MARIAN CALABRO

FOUR WINDS PRESS

New York

Lines on page 91 are from *Track of the Grizzly* by Frank C. Craighead, Jr.
Copyright © 1979 by Frank C. Craighead, Jr.
Reprinted with permission of Sierra Club Books.

Four Winds Press
Macmillan Publishing Company
866 Third Avenue, New York, NY 10022
Collier Macmillan Canada, Inc.
First Edition   Printed in the United States of America
10 9 8 7 6 5 4 3 2 1
The text of this book is set in 12 point Sabon.

Library of Congress Cataloging-in-Publication Data
Calabro, Marian.
Operation grizzly bear / by Marian Calabro.—1st ed.   p.   cm.
Bibliography: p.   Includes index.
Summary: Describes the twelve-year study of grizzly bears done
by John and Frank Craighead in Yellowstone National Park, in which
their use of the radio-tracking collar and other innovations added
to the scope of human knowledge about the grizzly.
ISBN 0-02-716241-9
1. Grizzly bear—Yellowstone National Park—Juvenile literature.
2. Craighead, John Johnson, 1916–   —Juvenile literature.
3. Craighead, Frank C. (Frank Cooper), 1916–   —Juvenile
literature. 4. Mammals—Yellowstone National Park—Juvenile
literature. 5. Zoologists—Yellowstone National Park—Biography—
Juvenile literature. 6. Yellowstone National Park—Juvenile
literature. [1. Grizzly bear. 2. Bears. 3. Craighead, John
Johnson, 1916–   . 4. Craighead, Frank C. (Frank Cooper), 1916–
5. Yellowstone National Park.] I. Title.
QL737.C27C35 1989 599.74′446—dc19 88-37497 CIP AC
Map by Andrew Mudryk

ACKNOWLEDGMENTS

First and foremost I thank Frank C. Craighead, Jr., and John Craighead, who understand the importance of books for young readers and who gave generously of their time and knowledge as I wrote this one. They helped immeasurably by lending reference materials and providing photographs. I am particularly indebted to *Track of the Grizzly* by Frank C. Craighead, Jr., for the organization of information in chapters 5–8 of this book. Most of all, I am grateful to Frank and John for agreeing to be interviewed about their grizzly bear study. All quoted material herein, except as noted, is taken from those interviews.

I also thank everyone who offered hospitality and insights during my visits to the Craigheads in Wyoming and Montana: Frank's wife, Shirley, and his son Lance; John's wife, Margaret, and their sons, Derek and John; and the staff of the Craighead Wildlife–Wildlands Institute.

Special gratitude goes to Jean Craighead George, whom I did not meet but whose autobiography, *Journey Inward,* ignited my curiosity about her "family of naturalists."

Thanks also to fellow author Thomas McNamee, who previewed the latest official data on Yellowstone grizzly recovery as this book was going to press.

While Frank Craighead did review the manuscript for factual accuracy, I wish to emphasize that the final account of "Operation Grizzly Bear" is strictly my own.

Finally, for fine editing and moral support, I thank Cindy Kane and Bernie Libster.

To the memory of my father

John Calabro

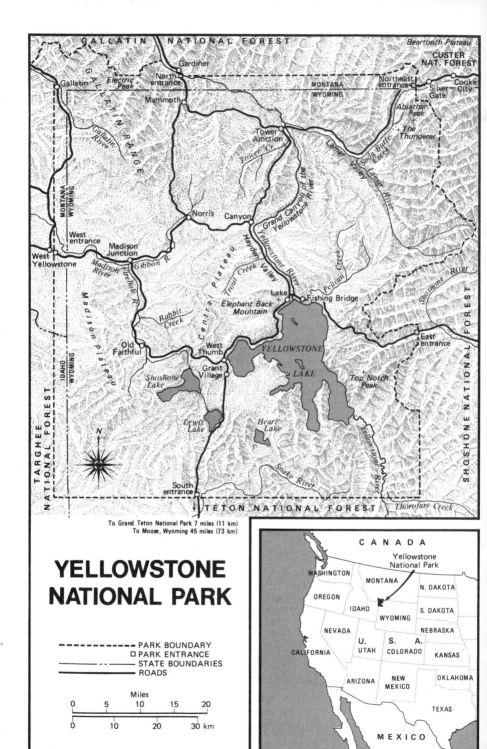

YELLOWSTONE
NATIONAL PARK

--------- PARK BOUNDARY
□ PARK ENTRANCE
————— STATE BOUNDARIES
————— ROADS

Miles
0   5   10   15   20
0   10   20   30 km

To Grand Teton National Park 7 miles (11 km)
To Moose, Wyoming 45 miles (73 km)

CONTENTS

CHAPTER ONE

Introducing
"Operation Grizzly Bear"

Frank and John Craighead came to Yellowstone National Park in 1959 to study grizzly bears. By 1971, when they left, they knew just about all there is to know about grizzlies.

In 1959, the Craigheads—identical twin brothers—were already well-known wildlife scientists. They had done major studies of the hawks and owls, elk, and coyote, and they were ready for a new challenge. For years they had talked about working together on a big project, one that would make a difference in the world of wildlife.

They knew that *Ursus arctos horribilis,* as the

grizzly bear is classified scientifically, had been named an endangered species: one in danger of becoming extinct. But for the most part, the grizzly was a mystery. How did it live? Why did it die? There were plenty of stories but surprisingly few facts. Most people knew only that the great bear was in trouble.

Together, the Craigheads formed the idea of a new, joint project. Its purpose was as bold as it was simple: to gather the kind of information that could help save the endangered, magnificent grizzly bear.

From the dawn of time until the 1800s, grizzlies had never needed help. They had no enemies. American Indians hunted them, but mostly as a test of strength. It took as many as ten Indians to kill a grizzly, and often a few hunters would die in the battle. The victors tore out the grizzly's heart and ate it raw. They hoped to assume the strength and courage of the hump-necked bear with the silver-tipped fur.

Held sacred by most Indian tribes, grizzlies reigned from the Pacific Ocean east to the Mississippi River; from the Arctic Circle south to Mexico. Then white settlers came and the balance changed. These settlers made inroads on the wide open spaces that were the bear's territory. And they invented the one weapon that gave man an advantage over the silvertip, as the grizzly was nicknamed.

"The Rapid Fire Rifle—Loads Itself—Big Enough for the Biggest Game" was the promise of a 1907 advertisement for Remington Autoloading Rifles. The art for the ad showed a cowboy trapped on a ledge by a snarling grizzly. (It was inaccurate, because grizzlies can't snarl. They don't have the right kind of lip muscles.)

The repeating rifle spelled instant death to all kinds of predators that stood in the way of settlers' farms, ranches, homes, and towns. Black bears, coyotes, foxes, and wolves all fell victim to the quest for progress.

Grizzlies were hit especially hard. Once they had roamed freely, by the thousands, through the American West. In the early 1800s there were probably ten thousand silvertips in California alone. In the 1850s, James Capen "Grizzly" Adams, an animal tamer and showman, brought grizzlies down from the Sierra Mountains and exhibited them in San Francisco. But by 1924, hunters had killed the last California grizzly.

By the 1950s fewer than one thousand grizzlies lived in the lower forty-eight states. Most survived on protected lands in Yellowstone National Park, which extends through parts of Wyoming, Montana, and Idaho, and outside park borders in those states. The only other sizable population was in Glacier National Park in northern Montana.

But even "protected" habitat was threatened. Tourists were pouring into Yellowstone and Glacier. To serve them, new roads and campgrounds were created. So grizzlies ranged throughout the National Forest areas that surround the parks. Unlike national parks, national forests can be used for logging, hunt-

Grizzly bears in Hayden Valley, Yellowstone National Park

FRANK C. CRAIGHEAD, JR.

ing, and livestock grazing. Those uses don't mix well with grizzlies.

The grizzly was losing ground. People were invading more and more of the bear's open spaces, causing the grizzly population to dwindle at an alarming rate. But before the bears could be helped, scientists had to learn more about them. And by the late 1950s they finally had the tools to study them effectively.

In 1944, biologist Olaus Murie had done the first formal study of bears in Yellowstone. Because tourists were scarce during the World War II years, it was easy to observe wildlife in the park. But that was all Dr. Murie could do—observe bears from afar, mostly at the dumps where they fed.

Before a bear can be studied up close, it must be immobilized. A young scientist named Albert W. Erickson tried to do that in 1952. The process was primitive.

First the bear was trapped by the foot. Then the angry animal had to be tranquilized by an ether mask thrown over its face. Erickson wrestled with more than one hundred bears in just this way. Several of them died or were injured. Some of Erickson's helpers were hurt as well.

A few years later, capture guns were developed, along with anesthetics especially for animal use. A researcher could safely knock out a wild animal in order to tag and mark it.

The time was right for a full-scale study of grizzlies. Frank Craighead had experimented with capture equipment and anesthetics himself while working as manager of the Desert Game Range in Nevada. In 1957, he and John began to write proposals outlining their project.

In scientific terms, the Craigheads spelled out exactly what they planned to learn about grizzly bears in Yellowstone. How big was the population? Was it growing, shrinking, or holding its own? How young and how often did grizzlies breed? How were they born? What factors caused them to die?

These questions raised many more. The proposals also asked: How much space did silvertips need? What were their seasonal movements? Their feeding habits? What happened when they hibernated? And how did they behave around humans?

"Our goal was to find out how grizzlies live, and to use that knowledge so they might continue to live," John says. "It takes time, effort, and dedication to study an animal. It makes sense to use that information to help manage and protect it."

The Craigheads knew it would take a long time to profile the Yellowstone grizzly population and see how it changed. At the beginning they expected the study to take ten years. Inside and outside the park, it would last closer to fifteen. But if anyone could uncover the secrets of grizzly bears, Frank and John Craighead were the ones. In a way, they had been preparing for this project all their lives.

CHAPTER TWO

Introducing Frank and John Craighead

Frank C. Craighead, Jr., and John J. Craighead were born on August 14, 1916, and grew up in Washington, D.C., where their father was chief entomologist for the U.S. Department of Agriculture. Dr. Frank C. Craighead, Sr., traveled the country to solve insect problems that threatened forests. He was known for his integrity and honesty.

"He was a model for us," John says. "He taught us there's only one right way in science, and that is to pursue the truth."

The twins' sister, Jean, has commented that a love-of-nature gene seems to run in the family along with fair hair and blue eyes. Nine generations of Craigheads have been naturalists. Frank, John, and Jean grew up learning the names of animals and plants. Although they lived in Washington during the school year, their parents often took them on camping weekends and outings along the remote reaches of the upper Potomac River.

Summers were a special time. While at the family's two-hundred-year-old homestead in rural Pennsylvania, the children practically lived outside in acres of fields, woods, and streams. Cousins and friends flocked around Frank and John, who always thought up the best adventures.

One adventure was falconry, a sport in which hawks are trained to hunt small game. The boys discovered this foreign "sport of kings" in an old issue of *National Geographic*. At age fourteen they helped to bring falconry to America.

Always ready to climb trees, Frank and John also spent their teenage years scaling the cliffs of the Potomac in search of duck hawks' nests. Their Washington backyard looked like a parking lot for birds of prey. Sparrow hawks, Cooper's hawks, and horned owls were tethered to perches by leashes and leg straps known as jesses. On weekends and in summer, the young falconers took off for the river and fields.

Their sister, Jean, three years younger, often tagged along. Her brothers teased her sometimes, but they also treated her as an equal. They gave her a hawk and taught her falconry. She held the reflectors while her brothers photographed birds in the wild, and she made her own sketches as they worked.

Years later Jean Craighead George wove these experiences into her popular books for young readers. There's more than a bit of Frank and John—and Jean—in Sam Gribley, the falconer who survives on his own in *My Side of the Mountain.* Jean looked at falconry from a girl's point of view in *The Summer of the Falcon.*

Like many identical twins, Frank and John shared most interests. "We have always done things together, getting sick at the same time being no exception," they told the *Saturday Evening Post* at age twenty-four, in an introduction to an article on wildlife photography written by Frank. They were alike in other ways, too, they noted: "We are so nearly identical in weight, height, and build, that our wrestling coach [at Pennsylvania State University] never knew which of us was which, and consequently we took turns entering meets."

The twins were accomplished writers and wildlife photographers at a young age. Their first book, *Hawks in the Hand,* was published the year they graduated from college. Their first *National Geographic* article, "Adventures with Birds of Prey," had appeared two years earlier. It began a long and happy connection with the National Geographic Society, which provided about half the funds for the grizzly bear study. Millions of fans have followed the Craigheads' work in *National Geographic* articles and

TV specials. In fact, it was the introduction to one of those articles that nicknamed the Yellowstone study "Operation Grizzly Bear."

That first *National Geographic* story led to an amazing friendship. It caught the attention of a fellow falconer, a young Indian prince called Bapa, who subsequently visited Frank and John at Penn State. After college graduation the twins got an assignment from the magazine to visit Bapa's homeland. That summer they lived as the prince's guests in Bhavnagar, north of Bombay on the Arabian Sea.

A car and driver were at their disposal. They joined Bapa for long days of hunting with trained hawks and cheetahs. At his brother's royal wedding they ate rice dusted with silver and gold. "Sometimes we'd just shake our heads and laugh," John recalls. "It was another world."

Coming home took thirty days because the Mediterranean route was closed to passenger ships. War was brewing in Europe on land and sea. With one eye on the world situation, Frank and John earned their master of science degrees in one year at the University of Michigan. Further education would have to wait. America entered World War II when the Japanese bombed Pearl Harbor in December 1941, and the Craigheads entered the Navy.

They were assigned as survival trainers in the Pacific, and the work suited them perfectly. The brothers were dropped onto desert islands and left to fend for themselves. From island natives they learned how to find hidden sources of food and water. The result was a training program that showed Navy pilots how to save their own lives if they found themselves stranded in the seas off Japan.

Frank and John liked survival training work enough to resume it after the war. But first they returned to the University of Michigan for the Ph.D. degrees that made them full-fledged wildlife biologists. And along the way, each man married and started a family.

The brothers still shared similar interests, but they lived and worked apart. John joined the University of Montana as professor of zoology and forestry. At the same time he worked for the U.S. government as leader of Montana's Cooperative Wildlife Research Unit. He built his home on the side of a mountain just outside Missoula, Montana.

Frank continued survival training and other projects at the U.S. Department of Defense in Washington. But he preferred to work in the outdoors, and he left to direct the Desert Game Range in Nevada for a few years. He also joined the staff of the State University of New York at Albany and set up his own Environmental Research Institute in Moose, Wyoming. Through the university and the institute, he worked with students in Wyoming.

John and Frank had both built log cabins in Moose after the war, and they returned to them whenever they could. The small buildings stood side by side, facing the jagged Grand Teton peaks and the fast-flowing Snake River. Yellowstone was forty-five miles north. The Jackson Hole valley teemed with birds, wildlife, and some of the world's best fishing. This was Craighead heaven.

The brothers had loved the area for a long time. As teenagers they had driven cross-country from Washington to the Grand Tetons to search for golden eagles. For the New York Zoological Society they'd studied the region's elk and coyote there. The Yellowstone study would give the brothers a chance to work near their cabin homes in Moose as well as a chance to work together again.

The money to fund the project came through in 1958. It would pay for the salaries of the Craigheads and their staff, and buy the equipment that the scientists needed. The National Geographic Society, the National Science Foundation, and fifteen other organizations supported the study, mainly in the form of yearly grants. The federal government also provided a small portion of funds.

Frank and John remained independent scientists, not National Park rangers or employees. They began their work in Yellowstone in spring 1959 under a "memo of understanding" with park superintendent Lemuel Garrison, who was glad to have them. The Craigheads would be able to assist rangers in handling bears, especially troublesome ones. And Mr. Garrison knew their data could help improve grizzly management in Yellowstone.

The brothers lived mainly in Yellowstone in the

warmer months during the grizzly bear study. Their families spent each summer nearby in the cabins at Moose, often traveling to Yellowstone to visit and help in the study. John and his wife, Margaret—a park ranger's daughter and a fine outdoorswoman—had three children: Karen, Derek, and John. Frank and his wife, Esther, were also the parents of three: Lance, Charlie, and Jana.

"Every year, when school ended, we'd pack up and off we'd go to Moose," the younger John Craighead remembers. "We'd be back and forth between the cabins and the park all summer long. Those were great times." Like his cousin Jana, John was about five years old when the study began in 1959. The older children were about twelve and ten. Another generation of Craigheads was growing up camping, fishing, backpacking, and filming and photographing wildlife. For them, as Karen Craighead later said, Yellowstone National Park was "a 2.25-million-acre backyard."

The study was headquartered in Canyon laboratory, a big, old, wooden building. No test tubes or jars of formaldehyde could be found there. The lab was filled with long wooden tables, maps, data form sheets, and files. Citizen band radios, headsets, speakers, antennas, and receivers were all around. Imprints of bear paws adorned the walls.

With bunkrooms full of sleeping bags and cots, the lab resembled a summer camp at times. Almost everyone working in the study stayed here. Often as

FRANK C. CRAIGHEAD, JR.

*John Craighead at work in Canyon
laboratory, the study headquarters,
plotting a grizzly bear's range*

many as twelve or fifteen scientists and assistants were on hand. Many were graduate students from New York and from John's program at the University of Montana—those doing field work to get their degrees. Spending a spring, summer, or fall in Yellowstone was their idea of the best way to earn credit.

The Canyon lab kitchen was big enough to prepare food for a small army. In fact, the building started life as a mess hall. During the Great Depression of the 1930s, it was used by the Civilian Conservation Corps, or CCC, a government program that put unemployed people to work in the outdoors. Thousands of CCC workers had eaten there.

Outdoors at the back of the lab, ropes dangled from the rafters. The assistants had to shin up and down them before dinner was served; they had to stay fit to work with grizzly bears. If an angry grizzly charged, a researcher had better be able to climb a tree to safety—fast.

No grizzlies were kept at the lab; the scientists observed and studied them in the open. But occasionally an orphaned cub or a campground troublemaker was held there overnight in a trap. Grizzlies who menaced tourists were trucked off and released by rangers into the backcountry.

Yellowstone has plenty of backcountry: over two million acres' worth. The park is a high-altitude plateau with relatively few roads and dozens of mountains with descriptive names such as Fortress, Electric, Elephant Back, The Thunderer, and Top Notch. Three million acres of national forests surround the park. The entire area, known as the Yellowstone ecosystem, is bigger than Rhode Island and Delaware combined.

Despite Yellowstone's vast size, much of the study took place close to Canyon lab. Nearby to the south was the Grand Canyon of the Yellowstone River, with its spectacular waterfalls splashing down through walls of yellow stone. It was one of the park's most wild and inaccessible places.

Southwest of the lab, about an hour away by car, stood Old Faithful. Erupting into plumes of towering steam every seventy-eight minutes, it was the centerpiece of a geyser basin filled with bubbling mud pots and slimy green algae pools. Tourists flocked here and made it Yellowstone's busiest area, yet grizzlies passed close by.

But the richest variety of wildlife was on display just south of the lab, in Hayden Valley. Here bison, elk, moose, mule deer, black bears, and grizzlies gathered peacefully. A wilderness of open shrubland and creeks, Hayden Valley was the true center of "Operation Grizzly Bear."

CHAPTER THREE

Tracking, Trapping, and Tagging Grizzly Bears

Frank Craighead took up his large-caliber rifle and aimed. Bull's-eye!

Forty feet away, a grizzly bear whirled toward him. A dart hung from its neck. It had been shot with a hypodermic needle containing a drug that would keep it motionless for a short time.

Frank also had another kind of gun close at hand. When tracking grizzlies, he and his colleagues carried bullet-loaded firearms to defend themselves in case of attack. But after a year in Yellowstone, during which they had captured thirty-nine grizzlies, they still hadn't needed to use the firearms.

17

John and Frank ear-tagging a grizzly bear   LANCE CRAIGHEAD

Tracking, Trapping, and Tagging Grizzly Bears

The grizzly—a female bear, or sow—stood up and stared at the men. Her eyelids began to flutter. She dropped to all fours but could not run away. The powerful muscle-relaxing medicine was doing its job.

The Craigheads and two research assistants, Maurice Hornocker and Wesley Woodgerd, stood silently twenty feet away. When the sow had remained motionless for a few crucial minutes, John approached her and gently poked a stick inside her mouth. She didn't bite. "She's under," he said.

The men swung into action. The bear would be unable to move for only fifteen or twenty minutes—and she might be grumpy when she awoke.

The first task was to weigh the grizzly. This one was easy to handle, because she was small and light. The men rolled her into a nylon rope net attached to a scale on their pickup truck. They hoisted her up and took the reading: 175 pounds.

John nodded and smiled at his brother. When they first saw the bear, Frank had guessed that she weighed 180 pounds. The accuracy of his observation was very important, because the bear's body weight told the scientists how much drug to administer.

The relationship between weight and dosage could only be discovered by trial and error. But an error could be fatal to man or bear. If the dose was too small, the bear might wake up too soon and attack. If it was too large, the bear might become ill or even die.

John and Maurice quickly snapped a numbered

metal tag onto each of the grizzly's ears. John was especially fast because he and Frank had been tagging and banding falcons and other birds since they were boys.

Next, they pierced the bear's ears and looped red, white, and blue vinyl streamers through the tough skin. All tagged bears wore "earrings," with a different color combination for each bear so observers could tell them apart in the wild.

Frank lifted the bear's right front leg and brushed aside her beautiful, silver-tipped fur. He tattooed her with the number "40," being careful not to splash any of the indelible ink on himself.

Wes was busy measuring the bear. She was four feet, eight inches tall, small for a young female grizzly. He quickly made some other notes: footpads eight inches, neck circumference twenty inches, approximate age two-and-a-half years, general condition excellent. And he made a plaster mold of her right front paw. Her five claws alone were almost as long as Wes's fingers.

Frank glanced at his watch. Their work was moving smoothly, so he had time to draw a blood sample from Bear Number 40. The sample would be studied by Dr. Morgan Berthrong, a Colorado pathologist and lifelong friend of the Craigheads. Dr. Berthrong wanted to find out why bears, unlike people, are able to eat fatty meats without suffering from heart disease or high cholesterol. His research might help prevent these conditions in humans.

Next John and Maurice opened the grizzly's huge jaws. Using a special kit, they took a mold of her teeth, which were big and sharp enough to disassemble the tough carcasses of elk, moose, black bears, and deer. The tooth replica would later be used to help pinpoint the animal's age. Bears' teeth are like tree trunks: they grow a new ring every year.

Though the grizzly was powerless to move, she could hear the men's voices, feel their hands, and smell their scents. Soon she began to breathe more rapidly, then to growl. She tottered to her feet. The drug was wearing off.

Bear Number 40 rubbed at her eyes and looked around for her temporary captors. But at the first sign of her quickened breath, the men had returned to the safety of the truck. However, they stayed nearby to make sure that no other animal overtook the sow in her weakened state.

Experience had taught the grizzly trackers to be cautious, but they were not afraid. Like most bears that have just been released, Bear Number 40 wasn't really angry or dangerous. Generally, in encounters with humans, grizzlies want only to get away. That's why Frank always offered this reminder to new field assistants: "When releasing grizzlies, point them away from you."

A grizzly can run as fast as a horse, but under these conditions Number 40 just ambled away. The men watched as she disappeared into Hayden Valley. Her ear streamers, which didn't appear to bother her at all, flashed colorfully in the sunlight.

Next on the agenda was Bear Number 41.

The Craighead brothers and their colleagues drove a few miles north of Canyon lab. They stopped beside a strange-looking trailer in an open field. It looked like a huge tin can laid on its side.

This odd contraption, made from a steel culvert, was a bear trap. Several times a week, the scientists hauled it to a different location. They baited it with food that bears can't resist—honey or fruit juice, and raw bacon or beef. Then they opened the trap gate, set the trigger, unhitched the trap, and drove away. Usually a bear was waiting behind the trap door when the men returned the next day.

Bear Number 40 hadn't been trapped; she had been roaming freely near the road when the men shot her with their dart gun. But traps were the most reliable way to catch and study bears.

Sure enough, when Frank peered through a peephole in the side of the trap that afternoon, the amber eyes of a bear stared back. The angry animal lunged forward and flashed its claws through the opening. Frank jumped back just in time.

It wasn't necessary to guess at this bear's weight. Instead, the men rehitched the trailer to the car and drove it to level ground. There, with a portable scale, they weighed both trap and bear, then subtracted the weight of the trap. Grizzly Number 41 was medium-sized: 520 pounds.

John loaded the dart gun, poked it through the peephole, and pulled the trigger. Even at such close range, the dart's brief sting didn't upset the animal more than a doctor's injection would bother a person. Bears have thick hides.

In just one minute, the bear was still. That was much faster than usual. "I hope we haven't overdosed him," John said.

Normally, to avoid harming the bear, the scientists tried to give a smaller dosage than might be necessary. If the bear needed another shot, an emergency syringe was always nearby.

Wes opened the heavy, steel, trap door. Seizing the massive hind legs, the men slowly dragged the boar, or male bear, into the open. They began the familiar team process of ear-tagging, measuring, and tattooing the grizzly.

But they had tagged only one ear and made a tooth print when the silvertip started to growl. With a dizzy tremble, he even tried to sit up.

Frank reached for the backup syringe, but he wasn't fast enough. Suddenly the grizzly lunged at John but missed him.

Then the bear's attention was diverted. He discovered the tattooing equipment and sent it flying. He sank his fearsome teeth into the heavy metal box that held the darts and drugs, leaving holes that looked as if they'd been made by rifle bullets.

John took these few seconds to pick himself up and race toward the car with the others. But the grizzly was back on their trail immediately. The men had barely slammed the doors behind them when he hurled himself onto the car hood.

The men instinctively shrank back and raised their hands to their faces, except Frank, who faced the bear squarely as he leaned forward and groped for the ignition. Only the pane of windshield glass stood between them.

The grizzly grimaced, but fortunately he was still a bit groggy and uncoordinated. He tumbled to the ground as the engine roared and the car careened away.

Yet the pursuit wasn't over. With mounting strength, Bear Number 41 stood up and chased the car, getting close enough to take a swipe at the back end. Frank stepped on the gas, and finally the boar was left behind in the dust. By then, the team had a nickname for him: Ivan the Terrible.

Wherever they traveled, the team would have an impressive memento to show. Ivan had gouged a perfect set of claw marks into the back of the car.

Frank and John returned to Canyon lab to start files on Bears 40 and 41, recording all the data on preprinted forms as they did for all the bears they were studying. They added to each life history whenever they observed or captured a bear again.

The messy but vital task of retrieving Ivan's trap

fell to the assistants. They hosed down the trap to wash away the traces of sticky food and bear droppings.

Almost every day, someone at the lab checked on grizzly sightings throughout Yellowstone. Park rangers weren't official study team members, but they kept count of all the bears they saw, tagged or not. So did backcountry campers and fishermen, who were glad to let rangers know when and where they saw grizzlies.

Study team members also counted the grizzlies, marked and unmarked, wherever seen, as well as those that fed at the four garbage dumps within the park. In autumn 1961, after two-and-a-half years of census-taking and field sightings, the Craigheads had tagged 122 silvertips and had the first reliable estimate of the total Yellowstone grizzly population: 200 bears.

Behind-the-scenes work wasn't as exciting as trapping grizzlies, but the scientists never found it dull. Slowly, patiently, they were building a body of first-hand data from which they could draw conclusions.

Still, like the explorers and trappers of the Old West, the bear researchers loved to collect spine-tingling tales about the ferocious "grizz." The difference was that the scientists' tales—like that of Ivan the Terrible—were true.

CHAPTER FOUR

Bringing Wildlife Study into the Space Age

"**D**o you really think a grizzly will keep that thing on?"

Looking down at Bear Number 40, field assistant Harry Reynolds dared to ask the question on everyone's mind. Collars were fine for dogs and cats, but would a huge, free-roaming bear tolerate one?

It was September 1961, more than two years into the study, and if the answer to Harry's question was yes, the study of wildlife could change forever. For this wasn't just any collar. Bundled into it was a lot of apparatus: batteries, a transmitter, and an antenna. The collar employed the same technology that lets listeners switch on a radio and tune into local stations. By using an electronic receiver to tune into the bear's collar, scientists could keep track of the animal from miles away.

When the study began, tracking grizzlies by radio had been a distant goal. Simply being able to capture and color-mark the silvertip bears was a big step forward. By the end of 1960 alone, the team had tagged sixty-seven grizzlies and made over seven hundred daytime observations.

But the researchers knew they were missing a lot. Grizzly bears are most active at night. They wander far and wide through rough terrain, sheltered from sight in dense woods. And they hibernate in remote dens for almost half the year.

Radio-tracking, also known as telemetry, was the breakthrough the Craigheads needed. They weren't the first wildlife scientists to realize this. In 1954, Robert D. LeMunyan had concocted a crude transmitter collar and put it on a woodchuck. He hadn't been able to track the animal past twenty-five yards—not much help where far-roaming grizzlies were concerned. Further development and testing were needed.

So while John spent his winters analyzing biological data from the study, Frank turned his attention to telemetry. With the help of a friend and ham radio operator, Hoke Franciscus, he drew up some requirements for a transmitter-collar system that could be used to track grizzlies in mountainous country. They looked something like this:

Range: Ideally, each collar needed to broadcast silent signals that could be picked up from ten to twenty miles away with long-range receiving antennas, and from at least one mile using portable hand-held receivers.

A big receiver at the lab, wired to an antenna on the roof, would pick up the distant incoming signals and convert them into sound. Mobile receivers on pickup trucks would pick up the mid-range signals. Hand-held receivers would be used to close in on the bear in the field.

Life: The transmitter, batteries, and loop antenna in the collar should last at least six months, so that a bear instrumented in spring could be tracked to its den in autumn.

Size and weight: As small and light as possible.

Signal: A pulsed signal would be better than a continuous one. Each bear could be identified by its own special number of pulses per minute.

With these specifications expressed in technical terms, Frank contacted several electronics companies. Some weren't even interested. Others thought they could make a radio collar but that it would cost too much money. A few simply laughed at the idea.

Eventually Frank found a sympathetic ear at the Philco Corporation, a famous maker of radios and televisions. A public relations man there was fascinated. Grizzly bears sporting collars designed by Philco—that was certainly a novel way to put the company name before the public.

But Philco's interest turned from publicity to science once a few of the company's electronic engineers got involved. Joel Varney and Richard Davies plunged into the project with great enthusiasm. This kind of research opportunity didn't come along every day.

And so began a year of tests. In the electronics lab and in the field, trial and error reigned. The engineers worked on making the smallest transmitters feasible. The study team worked on attaching them to silvertips. Neither job was easy.

The Craigheads made twenty-seven attachment tests in all. Using dummy transmitters, they tried polyvinyl tape, copper and brass wire, and nylon filament similar to fishing line. Figuring that bears might be annoyed by collars around their big necks, they tried tiny under-skin insertions. The grizzlies managed to lose every single attachment within days or weeks.

Only one prototype collar was a success. It was a braid of synthetic rope worn by Bear Number 37, a yearling who had been tagged with his family in 1960. Number 37 was the ideal test bear, young and frisky. Frolicking with his brother and foraging for food, he gave the collar a year of hard use. The yearling was also growing fast: during two summer months he gained one hundred pounds. The expandable rope collar grew right along with him. It seemed indestructible.

Meanwhile the engineers were doing pioneer work on developing a tiny radio. Dick Davies's final design weighed under two ounces—a real achievement at a time when most radios were bulky and relied on tubes to operate.

At last the team was ready to test the transmitter collar. On the evening of September 21, 1961, they trapped the grizzly who would become the world's first "radio bear." When they checked the culvert trap, they were delighted to find Bear Number 40. Because they had captured her the year before, they knew she was shy and unaggressive—a good candidate for this experiment.

Bear Number 40 spent the night quietly in the trap, eating the bacon bait and sometimes sticking her nose out of the peephole in the side. Her captors went back to the lab and worked past midnight to finish her radio collar.

They dipped the batteries in rubber to waterproof them. Then they wrapped the battery pack, transmitter, and loop antenna with a strip of fiberglass cloth and coated it with varnishlike resin.

This claw-proof bundle of instruments, which would fit snugly against the bear's throat, was then wrapped with tape of different colors. Number 40 would have a bright red and blue collar to match her remaining ear streamer—she had lost the other one in the past year.

Early in the morning, the team returned to the trap and immobilized the bear. When she was inert, they dragged her out and weighed and measured her. She had gained 125 pounds and grown to five feet, five inches in the past fifteen months.

Then they began to attach the collar, adjusting it to fit around her twenty-eight-inch neck. Several adjustments were needed, and it was almost an hour later when Frank finally bolted the radio collar closed. Altogether it weighed two pounds—so light that the bear would probably never notice it.

But despite the collar's light weight and clever design, it wasn't working correctly. It should have been broadcasting a strong, pulsing sound. When team member Mike Stephens hiked up the valley with a portable receiver, however, he picked up only a faint electronic signal from the bear.

Working without gloves in the autumn chill, aware that each minute counted, the team checked everything. The antenna was connected. The coating was intact. The transmitter was tuned to the right frequency, one assigned to the National Park Service. All systems were "go." What was wrong?

Frank appealed to Mike over the walkie-talkie. "Is the signal any stronger?"

Mike repeated the bad news. "No good."

Bear Number 40 was beginning to breathe faster. To finish the job, they had drugged her twice. She was finally waking up. To tranquilize her for even a few more minutes would be risky.

The men did not want another close call with a grizzly. Gathering their tools and packs, they began to leave, frustrated by their failure. The collar rig *was* working—but not well enough.

The sow awoke fully and walked away. Suddenly

the walkie-talkie sputtered to life. "Hold on!" cried Mike, who was still up the hill. "I'm tuning her in!"

Lying on the ground, the three-hundred-pound bear had been blocking her own signal. When she got up and walked, her steady electronic *beep* pulsed loud and clear.

Beep-beep-beep-beep. Mike came charging back so everyone could listen to Bear Number 40's unique signal of seventy beeps per minute.

Later in the afternoon, Frank rotated the receiver's loop antenna. He found the spot where the signal was srongest, then weakest. This pointed out the direction of the bear. Sure enough, he looked across the valley and there she was.

Only the receiver could translate the silent signals into sound. The bear was making history, and she couldn't even hear her collar beeping.

Heavy snow prevented the team from monitoring Number 40's signals on foot that day. The swirling flakes seemed to swallow her up. But she could no longer disappear into blizzards or wilderness. As long as that collar kept working, the Craigheads would meet up with her again and again whenever they chose. It was a new era in animal study.

Around the lab, spirits were soaring, especially Frank's. He had risked two years of time, money, and effort on the radio collar.

To honor Philco's Dick Davies, the Craigheads named Bear Number 40 after his wife. The first grizzly ever to wear a radio collar would be known as Marian. Bear Number 37 became the second radio-collared bear in history. When his rope collar was replaced with a working one like Marian's, he, too, got a nickname: Beep.

In future years, Dick and Joel made radio collars lighter, longer lasting, and more powerful. "As the collars improved, so did the data," Frank notes. "But nothing ever topped the first thrill of seeing that sow as she plodded along totally unaware of our presence."

One reason the radio-tracked bears were unaware of their observers was that grizzlies don't see as well as humans do. Their eyes are close together, so they have good depth perception, like most animals that hunt. But their eyes are also small in proportion to their bodies. The Craigheads found that many silvertips couldn't identify a person beyond about three hundred feet, a fact that the study team made good use of in tracking the bears.

But grizzlies do have a phenomenal sense of smell. One scientist had said that the world smells as sharp to a grizzly as a dead skunk smells to a human; of course, it doesn't always smell as bad! To get close to a bear without the bear knowing it, the trackers had to walk into the wind so the bear wouldn't catch a human scent. And they had to move quietly, because silvertips also hear extremely well.

The radio-trackers used their hand-held receivers to help them calculate their distance from a bear. The

*Field assistants radio-tracking
a released grizzly*

FRANK C. CRAIGHEAD, JR.

closer they were, the louder the signal. It was crucial to lower the volume as they approached, so the bear couldn't hear them coming.

The team tracked bears each year. They usually stayed far back and watched the bears through binoculars. But they also took care to position themselves by trees that were easy to climb—just in case. As they learned early, it was all too easy to "jump" or startle grizzlies at close range.

Tracking Marian one day shortly after she'd been collared, Frank tuned into a strong signal that began to fade. That usually meant the bear was moving away. He and Maurice kept pace, following the weak beeps. Then, without any warning, the signal suddenly got louder—and Marian sprang up just forty feet away.

Huff, huff. A grizzly's warning is like no other sound. Marian peered at the men, who stood rooted to the ground. They were scared. Was she? Or would she defend her space?

The bear took off. She stopped and glanced over her shoulder. Her stare held the men transfixed. Then she blinked and ran away.

Marian had been napping, as bears do, in a day bed dug into the cool earth. Her bed was next to a fallen tree whose thick clump of roots had shielded the radio signal. When the men circled past, they caught the signal full force.

A grizzly's fight-or-flight zone is about one hundred feet. If an ornery one such as Ivan the Terrible had been jumped at close range, he probably would have attacked. But Marian seemed more surprised than angry, a sensible reaction to the people who were starting to pop up around her so often.

Marian's behavior showed once again that grizzlies don't stalk or fear humans. The bears prefer simply to avoid them.

And while wildlife scientists try not to anthropomorphize—to assign human qualities to animals—the Craigheads had to admit that Marian seemed to trust them. She sensed that they wouldn't hurt her. The respect was mutual.

"That day we realized there were two studies going on," Frank says. "We were studying grizzlies. And they were studying us."

CHAPTER FIVE

Following Foragers and Discovering Dens: Grizzlies in Autumn

Everyone knew that grizzly bears wandered far and wide in search of food and mates. But no one knew how far.

And everyone knew that grizzlies denned up for the winter. But no one knew exactly when or where.

Now those mysteries could be solved. Radio-tracking had given the Craigheads a much wider view of grizzly life. As John says, "Before, we felt like we were looking through a keyhole."

By tuning into Marian's radio and following up with visual observations, the scientists learned to "read" a bear's signals from afar. When the beeps got louder and softer, the bear was moving about. Depending on the time of day and the season, it might be foraging for food, eating, playing, or courting. When the sound was constant, the bear was standing still or napping. And when the signal couldn't be heard, as Marian had shown, the bear was probably napping in a depression below ground level.

When the signal came and went, the bear was traveling over hills or through densely wooded areas. The team was often close behind—driving to distant points, following on foot, or taking radio "fixes" from two or more locations in order to plot the bear's precise position.

On big maps back at the lab, a grease-penciled *X* marked a bear's whereabouts. Each bear had its own color code. By connecting the *X* marks, the Craigheads discovered how far silvertips roamed and how much space they needed to live.

Some bears were wanderers. Number 38, Beep's twin, was a good example. In fall 1961, Frank radio-tracked this young bear. He sighted him occasionally and also followed his path from clues the bear left behind.

That fall, Bear Number 38 was two-and-a-half years old. At this age many young grizzlies are experiencing their first autumn away from their mother, foraging alone and preparing to den by themselves for the first time. However, Beep and Number 38 had been on their own a year sooner than most other bears. They had been weaned early, at age one.

Obeying his instincts, Number 38 began looking for a den site and fattening up for his winter sleep. Moving from Hayden Valley, he swam in the Yellowstone River and munched his way along its banks. He stopped at Pelican Creek campground, which he remembered from earlier visits. This was a dangerous tactic. Grizzlies who are bold around people and food become problem bears—and problem bears usually end up dead.

But in Yellowstone's cool autumn, the campground was empty. The restless bear traveled up the creek, alert to the scamperings of mice, ground squirrels, and marmots. These are favorite snacks for grizzlies, and Number 38 dug for them diligently: the hump on a grizzly's neck is pure hard muscle that enables him to dig like a steam shovel.

In one spot Frank watched for an hour as the young silvertip dislodged rocks as if they were pebbles. The hillside looked like a crater on the moon. But one rock held firm, a safe shelter for a quivering marmot who escaped being eaten.

Number 38 roamed over Specimen Ridge, down into the Lamar Valley, and through the rocky, wet terrain that led to Soda Butte Creek. He gorged all the way, pulling up tuberous plants and woody roots. He also visited a forest of whitebark pines, where he had feasted on nutritious pine nuts the previous year. But whitebark pines don't produce a crop every year, and this autumn he went away hungry.

So the young forager devoured whatever he could

find—elk thistle, strawberries, even butterflies. He was growing round and soft with stored fat, but still he was hungry. He was so ravenous that he raked aside bison droppings and scooped up the insects beneath.

Soon new sounds and scents wafted his way. Bear Number 38 was leaving the protected area of Yellowstone. The Montana towns of Silver Gate and Cooke City beckoned. He scrambled down Abiathar Peak, crossed the highway, and nosed out some garbage cans behind a restaurant. The scent of rotting food, so sweet to a grizzly, lured him on to the Cooke City town dump. It probably reminded him of his favorite summer feeding spot, Yellowstone's Trout Creek dump. He gorged at the Cooke City dump for three nights.

With renewed energy, Number 38 headed east to the Beartooth Plateau. He was now more than sixty miles northeast of his summer haunts in Hayden Valley. Unaware of boundary signs, he entered Gallatin National Forest.

Yellowstone National Park is ringed by national forests: Gallatin, Shoshone, Teton, Custer, and Targhee. Parts of these five forests are untouched wilderness. But other parts are busy with logging and livestock grazing, because the main purpose of national forests is multiple-use agricultural-forest business.

Sheep were grazing on Gallatin National Forest lands when Bear Number 38 approached. He had never seen a sheep before. He killed one and ate it.

Grizzlies always remember where they have gotten good food, and they usually return. The young silvertip returned to the ranch the very next night. This time the rancher was there, too, and he was armed. One bullet took the bear's life. Two years later, his brother Beep came to a similar end.

Number 38 and his brother Beep were typical of those grizzlies who broaden their range by making long forages in the fall. Luckily, most of their fellow nomads were not as ill-fated.

Yellowstone's chief grizzly nomad was Bear Number 76, or Pegleg. A big boar with a telltale limp, he once roamed fifty airline miles in a week. Fifteen to twenty miles a day isn't a lot for a bear on flat or easy ground, but Pegleg rambled in rough country. He crossed the Yellowstone River twice and climbed down the near-vertical wall of the park's Grand Canyon.

Bear Number 14, known as Bruno or the Thousand-Pound Boar, was also well-traveled. John, Frank, and two associates tried pursuing him one September. Bruno's *beep* led them far from roads and human activity, until their supplies were almost gone. After three days and nights, he simply outpaced them. They turned back, but the huge silvertip went on. His lifetime home range turned out to cover about a thousand square miles—an area almost as big as Rhode Island.

Yet many other grizzlies were homebodies. Marian

Operation Grizzly Bear

*A mother bear and cubs
crossing Trout Creek*

FRANK C. CRAIGHEAD, JR.

certainly was. Because she was radio-collared for eight years, the Craigheads were able to plot her home range precisely.

Marian conducted her life within a small area of eight square miles before becoming a mother. Then her range grew as her cubs did. But she never required more than thirty square miles to live, in part because Trout Creek dump was nearby. There she and dozens of other grizzlies enjoyed an ample supply of food—tourists' leftovers. The dump drew so many bears that Marian was also assured of finding a mate there.

By plotting twenty ranges over eight years, the Craigheads discovered that a grizzly forages in one basic area year after year. Females and younger bears of both sexes don't usually stray far beyond that core area. Adult males tend to roam farthest in search of food, den sites, and mates. And all grizzlies share their ranges; they aren't territorial, like dogs and wolves.

The bears are able to return to the same area because they have a strong homing instinct. Beep and Number 38 proved this. Frank and John often helped the Park Service to transport these troublemakers miles away from busy campgrounds. But a few days later the cubs would return. A grizzly's keen memory draws him back to the places he knows best—a trait that leads to death instead of survival when bear and man cross paths.

Of all the discoveries made in the study, one of the most important was that very few Yellowstone grizzlies lived only in Yellowstone. Many of them roamed into the national forests beyond the national park borders. The Craigheads hoped government policymakers would take notice of this fact. Every additional piece of protected wilderness would help save the grizzly from extinction.

Radio-tracking a grizzly to its den proved to be more difficult than studying its range. Frank and John would have liked to track Marian to her den in 1961, but her first transmitter collar wasn't strong enough for that. The next year they fitted her with a more powerful model, designed by Joel Varney. Beep and Bear Number 96 sported them, too. Still, late in the season, the Craigheads lost track of all three instrumented bears.

The equipment failure was frustrating. There was nothing to do but to wait and try again the following year. This time the team put collars on eight grizzlies. It was a smart move, because by late October 1963, only one collar was transmitting. It belonged to Bear Number 164, a sow recently seen with a pair of two-year-olds.

On the morning of November 5, the signal began to fade. Was Number 164 moving to her den or traveling out of range? If the team didn't find out fast, they'd have to put off den-tracking for yet another year. They grabbed their hand-held receivers, jumped into their pickup truck, and raced south.

By noon, Frank, John, Maurice, and field assistant Charlie Ridenour were deep in the dense forest. The grizzly was still there, according to her radio transmissions, and perhaps her offspring were nearby. But the men couldn't spot any bears or dens. It was snowing hard, and fallen trees made hiking doubly difficult. They hadn't seen one footprint except their own.

Beep-beep-BEEP-BEEP-BEEP. Frank hurried to lower the receiver volume. He and Maurice had climbed a slope and were standing atop a tangle of logs. Was a grizzly below? It was dangerously possible. An angry bear, especially a mother with youngsters in tow, could be upon them in seconds. And there were no trees to climb to safety. The lowest branch on the nearest lodgepole pine was thirty feet above them.

Firmly gripping their guns, Frank and Maurice inched forward, not knowing if they were moving toward or away from the bear.

Then Maurice stopped and pointed downhill. Frank expected to see a grizzly, but instead he saw traces of dirt on snow at the base of a fir tree. The dirt had been thrown out when the grizzly dug her den. The entrance was a large dark hole in the hillside.

Turning up the receiver confirmed it: Bear Number 164 was here, in her den. Tracks extended a few feet beyond the entrance. The men moved sidelong for a better look. Frank put away his gun and took up his camera.

The bear knew they were there—Frank could feel it. She had retreated when she heard them coming. If they stayed longer, they might catch a glimpse of her. They might also invite trouble.

The team decided it would be best to leave. Buoyed by their success, they plowed energetically through the heavy snow. They still hoped to learn whether the mother bear was denning alone or with her two-year-olds, but for now they were thrilled to have found their first den.

Frank blazed trail-markers into trees as the party headed home. They were eager to see Number 164's den from the inside, and they planned to follow the markers back in late winter.

CHAPTER SIX

Studying Bears As They Sleep: Grizzlies and Black Bears in Winter

Yellowstone's fierce winter had blanketed Bear Number 164's winter home in snow drifts ten feet deep when John and Maurice followed the trail back to her den. The only sign of life was the bear's warm breath, which escaped in wisps and instantly evaporated into the frigid January air.

The men jumped up and down on the steep slope, struggling to pack down the snow. Finally they took off their snowshoes and used them to shovel an opening to the den. Their plan was to dart-gun the grizzly, take a blood sample, and attach thermometers to both the bear and her den.

John Craighead in the entrance to the bear Marian's den after she left it in spring 1965

FRANK C. CRAIGHEAD, JR.

From far within, the grizzly growled.

The men paused for a moment. They'd heard other bears snore or groan in their sleep. They went on digging.

Another growl came, louder now. John and Maurice sensed a warning. This silvertip did not seem eager to entertain human visitors.

The men knew they would be helpless if the aroused sow charged from her den. An immobilizing dart wouldn't take effect instantly. And, snowshoes or not, they couldn't beat a hasty retreat in ten feet of snow.

Face-to-face with the bear, the scientists' only option would be to shoot in self-defense. But they didn't wish to risk their lives, or hers.

John made the decision. "We'd better leave now," he said to Maurice. Left undisturbed, the grizzly would not awaken again until late March.

Winter was just beginning to yield to spring when the team returned to Number 164's den. The bear was awake and gone, off to the lower reaches of the park in search of elk carcasses and other good things to eat. The scientists were back to investigate the den.

Scattered around the site were remnants of snow caves with bough beds. The men saw that the caves were at different levels, which indicated that they had been formed at different times. The men guessed that in the early weeks when emerging from hibernation, the drowsy bear had made and rested on these beds.

New snow falling on top of her formed the caves. They were melting now, but some still had vertical tubes formed by the bear's rising breath.

The den itself was dug right into the hillside. Tree roots framed the opening, so entering was a tight squeeze. And the location was quite remote. In all these ways, the grizzly guarded against intruders during her winter sleep.

In other ways, too, Bear Number 164 was a smart architect. Her den's narrow entry captured the blowing snow, which acted as camouflage and insulation. Root support kept the den from collapsing. The whole structure faced north, so it wouldn't thaw during any brief warm spells.

Beyond the three-foot hallway was the bear's sleeping chamber. It was five feet long, four-and-a-half feet wide, and three feet high—just big enough for one curled-up bear and a bough bed.

The small size of the space confirmed an earlier guess by study team members. Bear Number 164's two-year-olds had not hibernated with their mother. By radio-tracking and observing, the Craigheads later learned that this is often the case. Once a grizzly is weaned—usually in the second summer or third winter of its life—it lives on its own. That includes foraging and denning by itself.

However, radio-tracking did prove that most one-year-old grizzlies share their mother's den. This makes sense, because yearlings are still nursing. Also, by watching and helping their mother build a den, they learn den-building skills for the future.

By tracking silvertips to their dens each autumn and returning to explore in spring, the Craigheads made many discoveries. They found that every grizzly den is as cleverly located and constructed as Bear Number 164's. They also learned that grizzlies almost always dig their own dens, instead of using ready-made caves, and that they seem to excavate new dens each year rather than reuse old ones.

But the brothers wanted to unlock more of the mysteries of hibernating grizzlies. How warm was a den? How deeply did a grizzly sleep?

Determined to find answers, winter after winter the team approached grizzly dens. Each time the growling inhabitants sent them on their way. Even placid Marian became annoyed when they came knocking.

The scientists had to face facts. The conditions were simply not in their favor. Yet they weren't about to give up. If they couldn't safely study *Ursus arctos horribilis* in winter, they'd study its cousin *Ursus americanus*—the American black bear, which hibernates in basically the same way.

Why would black bear hibernators be easier to study? First, black bears flee rather than attack if met at close range. Second, they are smaller and less powerful than grizzlies. An average male black bear weighs about two hundred pounds—an equal match for a husky human scientist. By contrast, most full-grown male grizzlies in the Craighead study tipped the scales at five hundred pounds or more.

In addition, the scientists could track black bears to their dens without radio-collaring them. Unlike grizzlies, black bears don't wait for blizzards to den up. Their footprints aren't erased by falling snow.

Black bears would also be better candidates for study because their dens are within easier reach. Grizzlies are long-clawed, and they dig their own winter homes on isolated slopes. Black bears, which have short claws, aren't good diggers, and they use natural caves or shelters instead.

So when the next denning season arrived, the study team was ready. John, Frank, Maurice, and Charlie Ridenour approached a black bear's cave den not far from Old Faithful. Like a grizzly, this black bear was a light sleeper. Their movements awoke her.

When the bear peered out of the den, John shot her with a tranquilizing dart. She complained with a brief bellow, then disappeared into her hideaway.

The scientists waited as thirty minutes ticked by. Had the drug taken effect? There was only one way to find out.

John inched into the den first. Frank and Maurice followed, while Charlie stood guard outside.

The tunnel seemed endless, longer than the entry to any grizzly den. Frank later measured it at fifteen feet. It was also horribly damp, because the bear had denned up near the warm springs of the geyser basin.

John called back to the others, relief in his voice. "She's unconscious. Come on in."

Soon all three men crowded into the small chamber. The bear took up most of the space. She hadn't bothered to make herself a bed of branches and sticks, which was no surprise. There was no need for insulation. This den was already stifling from the hot springs underground.

Now came the hard part. The team needed to roll the bear over to draw a sample of her blood. The only illumination came from John's flashlight. Elbows bumped against mud and fur as the sweating men struggled with the heavy sow and the big hypodermic needle.

As the men crawled from the den holding the hard-won vial of blood, the bear began to awaken and growl. John, Frank, and Maurice emerged into the bright sun, squinting and smiling at Charlie. Their first visit to an occupied black bear den had been a success.

Next the Craigheads wanted to record the temperature patterns of bears in their dens. This would help complete a winter portrait of the bear. And with America's space program in full swing, it might have other uses. The National Aeronautics and Space Administration (NASA) had its eye on bear studies. If astronauts could learn to mimic hibernation, journeys to distant planets might become a reality.

The first step in temperature recording led back to Joel Varney's lab. Drawing on his experience with radio collars, Joel used a special temperature-measuring instrument called a thermistor. No bigger than half a match head, it gave accurate temperature readings by radio over long distances when inserted under an animal's skin. John and Frank had tested thermistors on Yellowstone elk. By 1967 they were ready to attach one to a bear.

Once again, for safety's sake, a black bear was chosen for the experiment. The boar gave the scientists a good scare, however. Upon being dart-gunned, he rushed from his den and charged. Just as suddenly, he turned tail and disappeared over a wall of snow. Luckily the men found him after the drug had taken hold.

When the bear awoke, he wore a new radio collar with the pulse rate regulated by a thermistor. He was also in his den, snug in his warm bough bed, and the den temperature was being monitored by a radio as well. Getting the bear back inside had been a test of strength—even with four people to tug, push, and prod him through the narrow opening.

The scientists set up camp along the nearby Gibbon River. Here they were within range of the signals by which they could chart the temperatures of bear and den. They pitched tents, built a fire, and settled in for twenty-four hours of nonstop monitoring. Through the long hours of darkness they took turns with a radio receiver and stopwatch, counting the beeps per minute and converting the numbers into degrees of temperature.

On this and other field trips, the Craigheads learned that hibernating black bears have a body temperature of 95° Fahrenheit (35° on the Celsius scale), compared to the summer average of 101°F (38.3°C). They also retain their year-round pattern of warming up during the daylight hours, even while fast asleep in cold, dark caves.

Because summer temperatures and sleep patterns were the same for black bears and grizzlies, the team felt safe in assuming that winter data on black bears also applied to silvertips. Bears in general seemed not to lose much body heat during hibernation. This would explain why they are never far from wakefulness.

Because bears can be roused from their winter sleeps, a few wildlife biologists do not consider them to be true hibernators. They apply the word "hibernation" only to the comalike sleep of ground squirrels, woodchucks, marmots, and other small mammals whose winter body temperatures plunge to 40°F (4.4°C) or less. But most scientists, the Craigheads among them, do define bears as hibernating animals.

An odd fact about hibernation is that smaller hibernators don't sleep straight through the winter. These animals periodically awaken automatically. They do so every few days to eat, drink, and eliminate wastes. Then they sink back into their super-deep sleep.

The Craighead study confirmed that hibernating bears never eat, drink, urinate, or defecate during the winter. They live off stored fat and absorb their wastes. They wake up automatically if their temperature falls to 89°F (26.1°C). Once awake, they warm up quickly because their breathing and circulation speed up; then they go back to sleep.

The study team needed an alarm system, too—at least while monitoring bears for days at a stretch in subfreezing cold. They loved the beauty and stillness of the winter wilderness. But "after shivering around a campfire all night, we had visions of working in heated rooms while data poured in," Frank admits.

So the Craigheads began to explore the idea of radio-monitoring bears in their dens from afar. It was a logical step beyond direct observation and radio-tracking.

By fall 1969, the experiment was under way. With help from NASA and the National Geographic Society, the weather satellite Nimbus became the team's newest research tool.

The satellite belonged to NASA. It circled the earth hourly, gathering data. Seven hundred miles above Yellowstone, it read the temperature of a hibernating black bear and the amount of light in its den.

The data was beamed to a dish in Fairbanks, Alaska, then transmitted to the Goddard Space Flight Center in Maryland. It came to the Craigheads in the form of computer printouts, to be studied in the comfort of their warm winter offices.

Satellites could never eliminate the need for field trips. To monitor the bear studied in the satellite experiment, the bulky transmitting equipment still had to be hauled over long, snowy distances on skis. The bear still had to be dart-gunned and instrumented. A battery-powered system still had to be installed as a backup; this helped to prove that the satellite readings were correct. And satellite studies were expensive. They proved too impractical to be used again in "Operation Grizzly Bear."

However, space-age tracking had its advantages. It produced a constant stream of data, faster and more accurately than field-tracking. And it allowed researchers to monitor an isolated animal over long distances. For example, the Craigheads knew almost instantly when the "satellite bear" left his den, although they were many hundreds of miles away. They were alerted by the sharp drop in the temperature of his bed.

While writing a *National Geographic* article on their experiment, Frank and John mused over other possible uses for satellite-tracking. Nimbus might be a scientist's eyes and ears in remote areas like the Arctic, the land of the polar bear. Or it could help explain how sea turtles navigate thousands of miles in open sea to lay their eggs at a precise spot.

But those were ideas for other biologists to explore. The Craigheads were busy in Yellowstone. In winter 1968, Marian had given birth to her third litter of cubs.

CHAPTER SEVEN

Watching Mothers and Cubs: Grizzlies in Spring

Three tiny creatures poked their heads out of the den. Covered with fine brown fur, they resembled perfect teddy bears.

The cubs blinked and blinked. Their noses quivered; their round ears twitched. Their first months had been spent inside the den. Sun, snow, and sky were brand-new to them.

Marian stood nearby. Like her cubs, she probably felt overwhelmed by the world after her winter's sleep. And she was hungry. But first and foremost she was on guard—alert to the presence of other grizzlies, humans, avalanches, or any danger to her new family.

Grizzlies in Spring

The cubs—two males and a female—had been born in the middle of Marian's hibernation, sometime in late January or early February 1968. They were her biggest litter yet. Her first two cubs had been born in 1964, when she was six years old. In 1966 she had given birth to another set of cubs.

Was Marian asleep or awake when her cubs were born? Did she immediately groom her offspring, as cat and dog mothers do? No one has been able to see inside the den of a hibernating grizzly to find out.

But "Operation Grizzly Bear" did reveal many other facts about grizzly reproduction. The average female grizzly in the study had her first litter at age five. Then she became pregnant every three to four years throughout her life. The oldest grizzly mother observed by the Craigheads was twenty-six years old, although few silvertips (male or female) live that long. Most cubs are born in pairs, although triplets and single births are not uncommon. Quadruplet cubs are very rare.

Grizzlies and black bears are unlike other mammals in one special way. Adult females become pregnant during mating season, usually in June. Yet the fertilized eggs do not begin growing until the mother-to-be has fattened up and entered her den in November. This phenomenon is called "delayed implantation." John Craighead was the first scientist to prove this; he autopsied a dead female grizzly one autumn and found embryos the size of pinheads floating free in her womb.

59

Grizzly cub, three to four months old   FRANK C. CRAIGHEAD, JR.

Delayed implantation is nature's way of ensuring that cubs are born during hibernation. That is the ideal time, for then the mother bear has fat reserves and is safe from danger. Without delayed implantation, cubs would have a seven- or eight-month gestation and would grow big in the womb. Instead, bears weigh a pound or less at birth—a handy adaptation in a crowded den. And because newborn cubs are blind and toothless, they make few demands on their hibernating mother. All they want is milk.

When Marian was nursing her earlier litter, John and Frank had taken samples of her milk. Laboratory analysis showed it to be incredibly rich, with proteins and minerals and 50 percent fat. (By comparison, the cow's milk we drink is 2 to 4 percent fat.)

Cubs grow and thrive on this high-calorie diet. In fact, they hum with contentment when they nurse. "The first time I heard it, I thought I was walking toward a swarm of bees," Frank notes. "Then I saw a mother bear, sitting and leaning back like a rocking chair with her cubs suckling and buzzing away."

Marian's new cubs were no exception. They nursed at her six nipples every few hours through the day. In between feedings, they played. For hours on end they wrestled and romped in the snow. But if they strayed too far from the den, they got a cuffing. Grizzlies are strict mothers.

Marian and her cubs were still living off her winter reserves of fat. But there wasn't a lot of fat left on her. In fact, she looked almost skinny. After a few days outside the den, she gathered her cubs and started the pilgrimage downward to Hayden Valley.

All over Yellowstone, hungry grizzlies were heading for snow-free slopes. Spring food was more plentiful there. They foraged eagerly for green shoots of sedge pushing through the snow near the creeks. These greens aren't very filling, but Marian gobbled them up. Her cubs watched and did the same. They were quick to learn, and they remembered what their mother taught them.

Around this time, the study team fitted Marian with a new radio collar. It had become a spring tradition. The team members were thrilled to see her with a family of three.

One day, the wind brought news of a bonanza to Marian. She sniffed rotting meat—the best springtime smell of all to a grizzly. Her youngsters wanted to nurse, but she shoved them away. With the confused cubs scampering to keep up, she took off at a trot.

The scent led to the shore of the Yellowstone River. There lay the carcass of a bison, or buffalo. Weakened by winter, injury, or old age, it had drowned in the fast-moving waters. The dead body was prime food for hungry bears.

Other silvertips had gotten there first and torn open the tough hide. Marian dug into the stinking meat with gusto. Her cubs watched but didn't imitate her. They were still teething and couldn't really chew. That would change by summer, when each would have a full set of forty-two teeth.

Suddenly Marian stood up and looked around. A large male grizzly was on the scene, several hundred feet away.

Marian retreated, and the cubs did, too. They read clear warning signals in their mother's body language.

Marian had an excellent reason for being cautious. Four years before, in her first season as a mother, a male grizzly had killed one of her cubs.

It had happened with lightning speed. Marian's back had been turned while she dug for tubers to eat. One cub had stayed nearby, but his twin had roamed toward the woods. The huge boar had appeared in a flash and pounced on the little wanderer. Marian had raced to the scene, but the cub was already dead.

When grizzlies kill their own kind, it is always infanticide—the killing of a cub or yearling. The murderer is always an adult male grizzly. Sometimes he tries to eat the dead victim, but more often he simply runs away.

Such killings happen very rarely; the Craigheads observed only one other episode from 1959 to 1967. No one knows why grizzly infanticide happens at all. One guess is that it is a built-in population check. "More likely, it just can't be explained," John says. "Almost every population has its share of violent individuals who commit murder with no reason. The grizzly population seems to be no different."

Having learned from experience, Marian was ready to battle any grizzly—or human—who threatened her offspring. The Craigheads had seen her attack a boar and send him away bleeding. Perhaps the Yellowstone River grizzly sensed Marian's strength, for he kept his distance.

Soon mother and cubs followed some grizzly tracks uphill. Here they found hundreds of field mice and pocket gophers. Marian made a learning game of digging up mice and letting her youngsters catch and eat them. Sometimes a raven raced the cub for the prize, but usually the cub won.

On a menu of mother's milk, vegetation, and mice, the cubs grew bigger every day. Their antics kept Marian busy, but they also knew how to obey. Their lives depended on it.

John and Frank watched Marian closely as summer began, because she had done something odd with her previous family.

Normally, grizzlies are loners. They cross paths and share food, but they don't live in groups. Mothers drive their youngsters away when they are big enough to live on their own—usually at age two-and-a-half or three. Once a silvertip becomes independent, it shows no sign of recognizing its mother. And grizzly fathers play no role at all in family life.

But Marian had acted somewhat differently. In 1966, while nursing her second set of cubs, she struck up a friendship with another adult female, Bear Number 101, and her cub. Members of the study team had never seen anything like it.

The two grizzly families were inseparable. The

mothers searched for food side by side. The three youngsters played together every day. Sometimes the Craigheads went to observe Marian and found a storybook sight—all five bears bedded down together for the afternoon.

The scientists tried to find reasons for this unusual behavior. Most likely, it gave the young families an extra measure of security. But would they stay together in the fall, when silvertips start to get sleepy and like to be alone? How about during hibernation?

As the days grew shorter, the bear families continued to stick together. In earlier years, on their own, Marian and Number 101 had denned about sixteen miles apart. Now, instead of heading for their old areas, they chose a middle ground. Their dens were less than two miles from each other.

"More than anything, that told us these bears had a very strong bond of comradeship," Frank says.

And the surprises continued. Marian, Number 101, and their cubs kept each other company right up until denning time. One day, the Craigheads came to Marian's den with their movie camera and found all the bears outside. It was more than just a great scene to capture on film. "It had scientific meaning," Frank notes. "It showed that two adult bears could visit the same den without fighting over it."

The youngsters hibernated with their mothers, as cubs and yearlings almost always do. However, the two families did not den together. That would have been unusual indeed. Yet the friendship was not over.

After waking up in spring 1967, the grizzly families met once again. Marian left the meeting by herself. Number 101 went off with Marian's two yearling cubs as well as her own.

"We had seen sows adopt orphan cubs," John says. "But this was the first and only foster mother arrangement we ever observed." Had foster-mothering been the purpose of the bears' relationship all along? The Craigheads could not know for sure, but they had some ideas.

In scientific terms, Marian had always had a short reproductive cycle—two years. By contrast, most grizzly sows in Yellowstone mated and had cubs every three to four years.

By giving birth frequently, Marian helped to increase the population. More than anything, a high birth rate keeps grizzlies from becoming extinct.

However, to have a new family, Marian had to abandon the previous one. As long as she was producing milk, she would not mate. So, the Craigheads theorized, she would drive her year-old cubs away, while most mothers would wait until the cubs reached their second year. With her first litter, the young bear who survived was suddenly left on his own at the most vulnerable time of his life. Of all the cubs in the study, one out of three died before age two, usually of starvation or at the hands of hunters.

But through her friendship with Bear Number 101, Marian arranged for her second litter to be nursed and protected for an extra year. That improved their chances of individual survival. And Marian was free to breed again that year.

Mating season for Yellowstone grizzlies lasts only about three weeks a year. By mid-June, when the days are longest, it is at its height. Each year, the study team observed it from a distance in Hayden Valley.

Grizzly males compete for females. They fight so ferociously that many boars are scarred for life. This was how Old Scarface, Scar Chest, Scar Neck, Short Ear, and Cutlip got their names. "I remember hearing their battle roars from half a mile away," John recalls.

Most of these bears battled with Bear Number 12, the dominant silvertip, or "boss bear," from 1960 to 1965. Nicknamed "Inge" after boxing champion Ingemar Johansson, Number 12 won more fights than any other boar. This made him desirable to female grizzlies, so he mated more than the other males. His bold traits were passed on to new generations, helping to ensure grizzly survival.

Like all courting grizzlies, Inge had a romantic side. After winning a sow's attention, he would nuzzle and rub against her. She might ignore him for a few minutes, which made him even more attentive. After mating they would remain side by side for hours or days. Then another male would challenge Inge, and the cycle would begin again.

Marian was a favorite of Inge's. He was probably

the father of her first two litters, although both Marian and Inge had other mates.

By early July, male and female grizzlies were no longer interested in each other. When mating season ended, the single bears joined the mothers and cubs at the summer feeding spot they all liked best—the dump at Trout Creek in Hayden Valley.

CHAPTER EIGHT

Keeping Bears and People Apart: Grizzlies in Summer

"**W**here can we see bears?"

More than two million people visit Yellowstone National Park each year. That's the first question many of them ask.

Before World War II, it was easy to scc bears. Black bears lined the roads throughout Yellowstone, begging for handouts. People fed them and took photographs of the "roadside bums" from their cars.

With their natural shyness toward humans, very few grizzlies became beggar bears. However, from 1919 to 1941, tourists could watch grizzlies and black bears feed at the park's garbage dumps every day.

Grizzly and cubs at Trout Creek dump   FRANK C. CRAIGHEAD, JR.

Grandstands were even set up for good viewing. It was quite a show.

Those days are gone. Visitors today may not see one bear during a trip through Yellowstone. But they shouldn't be disappointed. There are good reasons for *not* feeding the bears—and for the National Park Service's policy of keeping bears and tourists apart.

Beggar bears may look cute, but they are dangerous. Conditioned to getting food from humans, they wander into campgrounds and threaten safety. Like Beep and his brother, these bears end up being relocated by park rangers. Often they head right back to the spots where they caused trouble, and usually they must be killed.

The dumps were closed to human onlookers in 1941. This kept the bears safely away from humans: they gathered peacefully to feed at dumps near Old Faithful, Trout Creek, West Yellowstone, and Gardiner. The paths to these areas were wide and well-worn.

When bears congregate, wildlife researchers are never far behind. In the 1940s, Olaus Murie studied grizzlies at the Yellowstone dumps. From 1959 through 1967, the Craigheads also used these areas—primarily to count grizzlies. They wanted to learn the total number of silvertips, with breakdowns by age and sex.

John directed this part of the study. Graduate students did the actual censuses, with occasional help from Derek, Charlie, and Lance Craighead. During days and evenings—as many as fifty times a summer—they watched the bears for three-and-a-half hours at a time. Sitting at a safe distance, they noted their observations, using standardized forms. It was important to record the data the same way from year to year.

Tagged grizzlies were easy to recognize. For instance, Marian's red-and-blue ear tags identified her as Bear Number 40. A quick check on a chart showed Bear Number 40 to be female, born in 1958.

Unmarked bears were trickier to identify. The observers had to be careful not to count them twice in one sitting. Usually they could tell the bear's sex from size clues: males are larger than females and have bigger heads.

Judging the age of an unmarked bear could be difficult. Usually, though, the census-takers could fit the bear into a general age class: cub, yearling, two- or three-year-old, subadult, or adult. And they had plenty of practice—one night in 1966 at Trout Creek they counted eighty-eight grizzlies.

All in all, the Craigheads counted an average of 177 grizzlies per year. They also estimated how many silvertips were *not* being counted at the dumps—about 23 percent. Their data showed that a likely total of 229 grizzlies lived in Yellowstone during the study.

Of the total Yellowstone grizzly population between 1959 and 1966, about one-third were cubs and yearlings. One-quarter of the grizzlies were ages two, three, or four. The rest were adults.

The Craigheads calculated that no more than 60 percent of the grizzlies in the study reached their second birthday. A few of the park's silvertips lived into their twenties or even thirties, but the average life span was only six years.

"Even when the grizzly population was at its peak, adult females were outnumbered by males," John notes. "The survival of grizzlies will always depend on whether those few childbearing females survive."

What caused Yellowstone's grizzlies to die? Over the first eight years of the study, hunting took the heaviest toll—about 45 percent of grizzlies who wandered outside of Yellowstone were shot. Within the park, problem bears had to be destroyed by rangers— that made up another 18 percent of the mortalities. The other known deaths were due to starvation, the elements, disease, or infanticide.

"We observed only one grizzly who seemed to die of just plain old age," Frank says.

Whenever they could, the Craigheads preserved parts of dead grizzlies for medical study by their friend Dr. Berthrong. In some cases they even saved the hides for museum display. As Frank puts it, "That way, if an animal had to be killed, at least some good came out of the death."

By July, good food for grizzlies is everywhere. Food is so plentiful that bears may feed for eighteen hours a day. This swaddles them in fat for the winter, and also keeps them out of the way of tourists when

Yellowstone is busiest.

The Craigheads learned a lot by watching bears gather and feed, whether at refuse dumps or elsewhere. In addition to counting grizzlies, they observed the animals' social behavior. Team member Maurice Hornocker paid special attention to this part of the study, because he wrote his master's degree thesis on it.

Whenever grizzlies are in groups, it is easy to pick out the dominant, or "alpha," animal—the "boss bear." It is always the most aggressive male. In mating season, he wins the fights and gets first pick of the females. While feeding, he gets first pick of the choicest food. Bear Number 12, Inge, was an alpha.

At the bottom of the social ladder is the "omega" bear. Most omegas are orphans, insecure and fearful. Some die in fights with bigger grizzlies. Those who survive usually avoid their fellow bears and become campground pests. Omega bears are doomed to a short life.

Most grizzlies, however, fall somewhere in between. "Beta" bears are one notch below alphas. These are other adult males, females with cubs, and scrappy younger males. One step down on the ladder, but not as low as omega bears, are females without cubs and docile young males. All these in-between bears fight for resources and do get their share—but never before the boss bear does.

If an alpha bear isn't around, the first beta bear on the scene takes charge. Frank saw this happen early one morning in 1963, when the *beep* of Bear Number 150's radio brought him to a hill in Hayden Valley.

Through the dim post-dawn light, Frank watched Number 150 as she tore into a carcass. Her cubs snacked on the rotting meat along with her.

Knowing how jumpy mothers with cubs can be, Frank stood under a tree he could climb quickly. He looked around and spotted Marian in the shadows of the forest.

Because she was not yet a mother at this time, Marian ranked low on the grizzly social scale. She seemed to be waiting her turn to eat. At one point she moved timidly toward the carcass, but she stopped. Frank had seen plenty of mother bears glare at their cubs with a look that seemed to say: "Stop what you're doing and wait right there." He thought Bear Number 150 might have given Marian the same kind of look.

Suddenly a third sow ran out of the woods toward the carcass. This female was far bigger than Number 150 and Marian. Her direct gallop indicated that she was fearless.

Number 150 and her cubs got the message. No longer dominant, they moved away. In their haste they almost ran straight into Frank, who swung up into the tree. The new bear realized he was there, and she also disappeared.

Finally the carcass was free. Marian edged toward it cautiously, ready to defer to any challenger. She nudged at the dead body with her shoulders, trying to get at the meat. But when the wind shifted, Marian caught Frank's scent and she, too, ran off.

Frank waited and checked his radio. By nine A.M. he knew the bears would be in their day beds. They wouldn't return to feed until early evening. He decided to come back to watch then. In the meantime, coyotes and magpies moved in for their share of the food.

Sure enough, Bear Number 150 and her cubs returned late in the day. They resumed eating. Marian stood nearby in a submissive posture—head down, taking only small steps. She seemed to be asking permission to join them.

After a few minutes, Number 150 signaled yes by stepping aside, and Marian approached. During the evening more grizzlies came around and showed deference to Number 150. They were also permitted to feed. Aside from a few short growls, the group ate together peacefully.

Grizzlies who fight over food or mates could easily kill each other. Instead, they cooperate according to their own social structure. "This way the bears don't waste energy," John says. "They concentrate on getting and sharing high-quality food that will sustain them."

Grizzlies are strong enough to kill people, but attacks on humans are rare. Since 1872, when Yellowstone was established as America's first national park, only five persons have been killed by grizzlies there. (A sixth person died in a Yellowstone bear attack, but the species of bear was not certain.) Of the 80 million people who visited the park from 1931 to 1988, fewer than one hundred were injured by silvertips. And in all their years of grizzly handling, no member of the Craighead study team ever had to shoot at a bear in self-defense.

In recent years, it has been safer to camp in grizzly country than to drive there. From 1978 to 1987, over 23 million visitors flocked to Yellowstone. About 5,600 of them required medical attention, mostly due to traffic accidents. Only thirteen were attacked by grizzlies.

Still, grizzlies can be ferocious and unpredictable. "Their temperaments seem to differ, depending on age, mood, and physical condition," John points out. "Hungry or injured bears may be irritable. Females with cubs are definitely quicker to attack."

How can visitors lessen the risk of attack? Grizzly experts offer these guidelines:

- Never surprise a grizzly. When hiking through the backcountry, make noise, talk, or even wear a "bear bell." The jingling sound will signal your presence and help to keep grizzlies away.
- Be extra-cautious in dense woods, where grizzlies bed down during the day. Avoid these areas, if possible. If you do hike through, ring your bell, talk, and whistle.
- If you see a grizzly, don't approach it. The

bear will almost always attack when startled or cornered, especially if met at three hundred feet or less. Instead, try to move so that air currents carry your scent to the bear. Most grizzlies will run away when they smell a human nearby. If you are not sure which way the air is moving, stand still. Face the bear or move slowly until the bear retreats.

- *Never* run from a grizzly. This triggers the bear's instinct to chase and catch fleeing prey. And no human can outrun a grizzly.
- Don't assume that a standing bear is ready to charge. Due to poor eyesight, grizzlies often stand to see better.
- If there's a sturdy tree nearby, climb it. Do this only if you can get at least ten feet up before the bear reaches you. And do it only if you think the bear *is* a grizzly: look for long front claws and a large hump above the shoulders. Grizzlies can't climb trees, but black bears can. Once in the tree, you'll have to wait for the grizzly to go away. This may take minutes or hours.
- If climbing is impossible, try to stand your ground. Do not provoke the bear. If it attacks, rolling up in a ball with your hands behind your neck—"playing dead"—may lessen injuries. Grizzlies kill primarily by biting the victim's neck and head.
- Never feed a grizzly. On the trail and in camp,

keep food odors to a minimum. Store all food and cooking pots at least two hundred feet from your tent, and never sleep close to where you've cooked a meal. Don't bury any trash. Burn all cans and food containers to take away their odors, and carry them out in a tightly wrapped bag when you leave the campsite.

• Read all information provided by the National Park Service or other land authority. Be especially alert for warning signs posted by rangers. Campgrounds and trails are closed to the public when troublesome grizzlies are nearby. Heed these warnings.

Following these guidelines will help to protect both people and bears. But very rarely, a grizzly will attack for what seems to be no reason at all.

In August 1967, two fatal attacks happened on the same night. Several hundred miles from Yellowstone, in separate places within Glacier National Park in Montana, two young women were mauled and killed by grizzlies. The gruesome killings made headlines around the world and became the subject of a book, *Night of the Grizzlies* by Jack Olsen, which is still a best-seller in Montana and Wyoming.

Reasons for the attacks were debated for years. The Park Service report noted that both victims were menstruating and wearing perfume, which may have spurred the attacks. There is no clear-cut scientific evidence for this, however. Some observers claimed that, unlike in Yellowstone, grizzlies in Glacier had been allowed to become beggar bears and had lost their natural caution around humans. Glacier officials denied these charges.

No matter who or what was to blame, one result was clear. The public was suddenly terrified of grizzlies. In response to the outcry, the National Park Service took another look at its bear management policies. It began to make dramatic changes that would affect every grizzly bear in America—including Marian and her cubs.

CHAPTER NINE

Leaving Yellowstone

The year 1967 was a turning point for "Operation Grizzly Bear." As John Craighead says, "That was when everything began to change."

The fatal attacks by grizzlies in Glacier National Park had caused an uproar. Visitors asked the same questions that Park Service officials asked themselves: Can attacks like these be prevented? Are changes needed in the way we manage wildlife, especially grizzlies?

The Craigheads had been thinking about these issues throughout their study. In spring 1967, a few months before the Glacier attacks, they had handed in the draft of a report called "Management of Bears in Yellowstone National Park."

Park superintendent Lemuel Garrison had asked for this report, as part of the earlier agreement that allowed Frank and John to work in Yellowstone. Since the park did not conduct its own grizzly bear studies, Mr. Garrison—and his temporary successor—were eager for recommendations based on the Craigheads' data.

But by late 1967, Yellowstone had a new superintendent and head biologist with their own views on grizzly management. They disagreed with Frank and John on many points—most of all on the closing of the dumps where grizzlies fed.

Park officials had been considering dump closures for a while. It was part of a plan to restore America's national parks to their original, primeval state. The policy-makers felt that in a true wilderness, nature should be allowed to take its course. For instance, they believed that forest fires in the wild should be left to burn and that grizzly bears should not feed on tourists' garbage.

John and Frank foresaw disaster if the dumps were closed abruptly. They warned that such a move was almost guaranteed to force hungry grizzlies into campgrounds.

The Craigheads pointed out that silvertips have always gathered wherever food is abundant. John later coined the name "ecocenters" for such places. Just as Alaskan grizzlies gather at the McNeil River to gorge on salmon, the bears of Yellowstone had included the dumps on their summer feeding rounds for eighty years.

"To grizzlies, garbage scraps are as natural as fish, rodents, berries, and roots," Frank points out. "When it comes to food, bears don't make a distinction."

Ecocenters keep bears out of trouble with humans. In Yellowstone, dumps had kept the animals far away from tourists. If the bears found the dumps closed, the Craigheads argued, they would forage nearby. In their wanderings they were likely to cross paths with campers, thus learning to associate food with man— a fatal lesson.

Was there a less risky way to wean the grizzlies from the dumps? John and Frank strongly believed there was. Drawing on their knowledge of the bears' feeding and movement patterns, they urged that the dumps be phased out slowly, over several years. At the same time, grizzly movement should be monitored. And other food sources, such as elk carcasses, should be used to draw the bears away from campgrounds.

"Closing these ecocenters meant destroying much more than a food supply," John says. He lists all the survival advantages that well-fed bears enjoy: larger litter sizes, higher survival rates for cubs, and faster growth.

But the new officials didn't see the need for eco-centers, or even for a period of adjustment. And the new chief biologist, Glen Cole, insisted there were plenty of "backcountry bears" never seen or counted in the study. As he saw it, some "garbage bears" might not adapt to the dump closings—but the "backcountry bears" would still survive.

John and Frank were dismayed. Craighead data showed that 75 to 80 percent of Yellowstone grizzlies fed at the dumps as well as in the backcountry. By ignoring this data, officials might force a substantial number of the park's silvertips into campgrounds. John and Frank believed the result could put the lives of visitors and bears at grave risk.

Because they were not National Park Service employees, John and Frank did not expect to be policymakers. But after eight years of scientific study and cooperation in Yellowstone, they felt they were being treated as "outsiders" who had no reason or right to speak out.

A battle had begun. At stake were the Craigheads' freedom of speech, the right to conduct independent research in America's national parks, and the survival of Yellowstone's grizzly bears.

Marian was ten years old in 1968. She had first trotted along the path to Trout Creek dump as a six-month-old cub at her mother's side. She had returned every summer since. Now she was there with her latest family, the three cubs born in January or February.

But in the summer of 1968, the bears got a rude surprise. The dump wasn't closed, but it didn't offer much to eat. Most of the edibles had been taken away to an incinerator. There wasn't much to be scavenged from what remained.

The food at the dumps had always been supplemental. Hundreds of grizzlies had counted on it for part, but not all, of their diet. So to get the same amount of food, they moved further afield. Meadows and forests surrounded the area. So did campgrounds. Canyon, Lake, and Fishing Bridge campgrounds were all eight miles or less from Trout Creek—a short walk for a grizzly.

Marian was never much of a wanderer. She had always found everything she needed within thirty square miles of Hayden Valley: food, mates, dense woods for napping and denning. But in 1968 she, like other grizzlies, had to expand her home range in search of food. She was especially hungry because she was producing milk for three growing cubs.

With or without cubs, Marian had always been a cautious bear. She had never set foot in a campground. And she managed to steer clear of them in 1968.

Yet the Craigheads' fears were becoming reality. Records for 1968 showed a sharp rise in campground visits by grizzlies. Some of these bears were trapped and moved from the area, or sent to zoos. Others were killed. When a grizzly was relocated or killed, the Park Service called it a "control action."

How many control actions had actually taken place? According to Frank, who had access to rangers' records, there were eighty-four grizzly control actions at Lake campground in 1968. According to official year-end summaries, there were twenty-four. In any case, the number of close calls had risen drastically. Park records showed nine grizzly incidents at Lake campground the year before.

Throughout the park, the situation grew worse. Frank was told by rangers that eight or nine grizzlies came into Canyon campground on one night. Snares were set—a type of trap that could harm visitors and invite lawsuits, in Frank's opinion. His warnings about the snares were unheeded.

Rangers had their hands full, especially those who were new to Yellowstone and unused to handling bears. Study team members had always helped rangers in the past. But starting in 1968 they were forbidden to do so.

For rangers who were sensitive to the bears' plight, the job was twice as hard. At least one felt that too many grizzlies were being killed needlessly. Ex-ranger Harry Reynolds, Jr., who became a study team member after retirement, later told the National Academy of Sciences that this was the unspoken park policy: " 'Take care of your problem bears at the local level in your own way; we don't need to hear about it at park headquarters.' "

At this point, the Craigheads were regarded as the world's foremost experts on grizzly bears. Their articles had appeared in dozens of magazines and scientific journals. With all the furor about the bears, it was natural for the press and public to seek out their opinions.

Obviously Frank and John clashed with the Park

Service on many aspects of bear management. Their reaction to the official report on the Glacier deaths was one example. In their opinion, the Park Service was to blame for allowing Glacier grizzlies to be fed by visitors.

In July 1968, Glen Cole visited Canyon laboratory to talk with Frank and other study team members. "Cole insisted that we were to give out the information in the official Glacier Report when questioned by the public," Frank wrote in his notebook at the time. "And he went further to state that if we did not do this they would see that we were pushed out of Yellowstone."

Frank's reply was that he and John did not wish to cause trouble for the Park Service. But neither did they intend to follow Dr. Cole's request. If questioned, they would base their comments only on their own research.

Not long after, the brothers learned that their headquarters, Canyon laboratory, would be bulldozed that fall. The Park Service claimed the old wooden building had to be razed for Yellowstone's 100th anniversary celebration four years later.

By written agreement, the Park Service had to provide lab space and housing for the study. Vacant buildings were available in other parts of the park. But when the Craigheads asked to use them, the Park Service did not comply. Undaunted, the brothers moved their equipment to a house trailer. According to Frank, they were soon "pressured" to move the

FRANK C. CRAIGHEAD, JR.

The bear Marian, immobilized and radio-collared. She was radio-collared each year from 1961 to 1969.

trailer off park property. They next set up headquarters in West Yellowstone, Montana, the first town beyond the park's western entrance. It was a three-hour round-trip drive from Canyon and Hayden Valley.

Work continued as best it could throughout 1968. Study team members tracked Marian to her den that fall. Bear Number 40 had become very special to them, and they were relieved that she and her cubs had survived the difficult year.

But 1969 was even more difficult. When the team came to Yellowstone in the spring, they were forbidden to tag, trap, or radio-collar any grizzlies. And rangers were under orders to remove ear tags and collars on all grizzlies they handled.

Frank says he was told that the markers were unnatural and an eyesore to tourists who might see the bears. When questioned later by the National Academy of Sciences, park officials claimed that "conspicuous markers are unnecessary for censusing or other research" because grizzlies can be identified by their looks.

The new rule was a crippling blow. Without the use of ear tags and radio collars, the Craigheads could no longer keep track of the grizzlies. Park officials couldn't do so either, as John pointed out. He argued that visual identification alone isn't scientifically accurate, and noted that Yellowstone still allowed black bears and elk to be marked for study purposes. But park officials stood firm.

Operation Grizzly Bear

Meanwhile, Yellowstone was nearing a state of crisis. In June 1969, a five-year-old girl was mauled by a grizzly at Fishing Bridge campground. In July, two young men were attacked by silvertips at Fishing Bridge.

National Park Service authorities in Washington, D.C., stepped in. They called for a special two-day September meeting in Yellowstone on bear management. Yellowstone officials were on hand, as were members of a special Park Service committee on the natural sciences. So were Frank, John, and other independent scientists.

Armed with information from the study, John Craighead spoke out against the dump closures. He also warned that the Yellowstone grizzly population was likely to die out altogether if killings continued at the 1968–1969 rates.

But officials looked on the Craigheads' research as suggestions, and they pursued their own policy. In October 1969, Rabbit Creek dump was closed.

That month, Marian came into a campground for the first time in her life. She and her yearlings had survived a busy and dangerous summer. But there was a lack of berries and pine nuts that fall, and they were hungry.

Marian and her family entered Lake campground on October 10. Two of her three youngsters were trapped there and released elsewhere. On October 13 at 7:30 A.M., she and the third yearling were spotted again. The ranger on duty dart-gunned the yearling.

In doing so, he placed himself in the worst possible position—between mother and cub.

Frank Craighead tells the rest of the story in his book, *Track of the Grizzly.* "As might have been expected, Marian came out of the woods at full charge. Just short of the ranger she turned toward her yearling, then pivoted back, as though uncertain of her next move. The ranger did not hesitate. He shot Marian between the eyes with his .44 Magnum. As she turned he shot two more quick rounds, followed by two more to assure that she was dead. . . .

"With Marian dead and family ties fragmented, her young dispersed to fend for themselves. . . . The trio making up Marian's last litter were all dead by 1972. Number 188, from an earlier litter, has not yet shown up on our mortality list," Frank wrote in 1979. "Perhaps he is still alive. Perhaps he has sired a litter that will carry on within the bear population some of the characteristics of the bear Marian, a grizzly that had adjusted to man perhaps as well as a wild grizzly ever will."

John and Frank were determined to continue their study. At the very least they wanted to monitor Yellowstone's remaining grizzlies.

When their written agreement with Yellowstone expired in 1970, they were offered a new one. Under it, anything they said or wrote as scientists would have to be approved in advance by the federal government.

The Craigheads refused to sign the agreement.

They believed that their right to free speech, a right guaranteed by the U.S. Constitution, would be at risk. "We couldn't sign it and call ourselves scientists," John asserts. In 1971 they left Yellowstone for good. But "Operation Grizzly Bear" wasn't over.

"Scientists have a responsibility to present data and to speak out when a national resource is threatened," John says. In the next few years, the Craigheads continued to study grizzlies—and to speak out firmly on their behalf.

CHAPTER TEN

Leaving a
Scientific Legacy

"**O**peration Grizzly Bear" gave new life to the fight for grizzly survival—a fight still very much alive today. Concerned scientists and citizens questioned how the National Park Service had treated the Craigheads and the grizzlies. They demanded an airing of the facts, and their pleas got louder when a young man was killed by a grizzly near Old Faithful in 1972.

Finally, in 1973, the U.S. Department of the Interior, which oversees the Park Service, asked the independent National Academy of Sciences to step in. Six respected wildlife scientists were appointed to study the status of grizzlies in Yellowstone. The scientists weren't given the power to make policy, but they were asked to make recommendations.

Their findings, issued in 1975, praised the Craigheads' work: "While the grizzly is a difficult species to study, the information assembled in the fifteen years of research by the Craigheads and their colleagues, together with the shorter term efforts of many other workers, is a uniquely rich data bank. It is certainly the best available for a population of grizzly bears."

The report criticized the Park Service's efforts. "Estimates of bear numbers for 1971 to 1973 are based on hypothetical numbers and there are no data to verify them," it stated. "The research program carried out by the National Park Service administration since 1970 has been inadequate to provide the data essential for devising sound management policies for the grizzly bears of the Yellowstone ecosystem."

The report supported the Craighead view that there were not separate groups of "dump-feeding" and "backcountry" bears. It also recommended the use of tags and collars as vital to proper research. The panel was more optimistic than the Craigheads about the chances for grizzly population growth. But it also urged caution, advising Yellowstone officials to limit "control killings" to ten per year.

On the whole, Frank and John had been proven right.

It was a bittersweet victory. "The Craigheads stuck to what they believed and paid a very dear price," wrote Maurice Hornocker in the *Wildlifer* magazine. Maurice was now an experienced wildlife scientist himself, working at the University of Idaho. "Their research was stopped. A large segment of the profession ostracized them. They were criticized by many. Yet, on principle, they endured and never faltered in their position."

Being proven right couldn't bring Marian and the other grizzlies back to life. Between 1969 and 1972, at least 160 silvertips had died in Yellowstone. No one could know exactly how many were left—nor if there were enough females of breeding age to restore the population.

However, in sticking by their findings, Frank and John alerted Americans to the grizzly's plight. Thanks in great part to them, the issue became *how*, not *if*, the bear should be protected. "One result of our study was that plenty of government money became available to study the grizzly," John notes.

Since the 1970s many people have studied grizzlies, using methods introduced by the Craigheads. The Yellowstone Interagency Grizzly Bear Study Team was created at the recommendation of the National Academy of Sciences. It brings together scientists from the federal government and state agencies of Wyoming, Montana, and Idaho. Montana has its own Border Grizzly Project. A federal Grizzly Bear Recovery Plan has been issued, but some states and parks still prefer to follow their own plans.

But studies alone can't save the grizzly. More than

anything, bears need wilderness. And their open space is being usurped for many other things.

Logging, mining, oil drilling, building ski resorts—these activities still go on in bear country near the national parks. The U.S. Forest Service has talked about replacing backwoods campsites with big commercial places run by Kampgrounds of America or Walt Disney. Even within Yellowstone, a huge tourist area called Grant Village has been built in the middle of prime grizzly habitat. Local people often favor such projects because they create jobs and boost the area's economy.

Everyone who studies grizzlies agrees that more open space is needed. If some silvertips could be relocated to the right areas, the population might grow. But while many people want the grizzly saved, very few want them nearby.

In 1985, Montana tried to find new homes for some of its grizzlies. State officials wrote to fifteen states, three Canadian provinces, and two of Canada's Northwest Territories. *Ursus arctos horribilis* had once thrived in all these areas. Would he be welcome now?

None of the American states wanted grizzlies. Only British Columbia would consider taking a few, since a small number of grizzlies lived there already.

The other big obstacle to bear survival is bullets. Grizzlies are no longer considered an endangered species; they were reclassified as a threatened species in 1969. (This reflected the U.S. government's belief that

grizzlies were not in danger of soon becoming extinct.)
Even as a threatened species they are entitled to pro-
tection by the Endangered Species Act, and under the
act it is illegal to kill grizzlies. Yet killings do occur.
Some bear killings are legal. Along with the problem grizzlies that must be shot, some have died while
being moved by helicopter. A few die from drug
overdoses during trapping and tagging.

In Montana, the only state besides Alaska that
allows grizzly hunting, up to fifteen bears can legally
be killed each year. The state believes there is a surplus
of silvertips and that limited hunting keeps the population in check. Some Montanans also argue that
hunted bears have a healthy fear of man. Many hunters in Montana see themselves as supporters of grizzly
bear survival.

Other killings, called poachings, are illegal. Poach-
ers can shoot a grizzly on the sly and sell its head,
pelt, and claws for thousands of dollars. Also, grizzlies
who wander onto a livestock ranch may face the own-
er's rifle. And in the wilderness, some hunters mistake
silvertips for black bears, which can be hunted by
quota.

Along with the usual methods of study, scientists
are trying new and different ways to save the grizzly.

Researchers from the University of Montana have
tried to "train" troublesome grizzlies. In closed areas
they set up mock campsites. When the bear comes to
investigate, they shoot it with rubber bullets or spray

it with foul but harmless repellents. The goal is to reduce the chance of conflict between bears and people.

John Craighead doesn't think much of these experiments. "It's our duty to modify our own behavior, not the bears'," he states flatly.

Many people are trying to do just that. The Great Bear Foundation, based in Montana, offers cash to ranchers who lose livestock to grizzlies. The payment is intended to cut down on poaching. And the National Audubon Society offers $15,000 for information that leads to the arrest and conviction of a poacher.

Given all these efforts, how many grizzlies are alive in the continental U.S. today? In Yellowstone, probably two hundred. In Montana, probably six hundred. A handful more have been spotted in Idaho and Washington.

A total of eight hundred or so grizzlies may sound like a lot. But in the past twenty years in these states, more have died than have been born. Current data suggests that the number of adult females is especially low. And if they die out, so will the species.

Many experts, including the Craigheads, say the Yellowstone grizzly is still in grave danger. According to their computer projections, so many silvertips were killed in the late 1960s and 1970s that the population may continue to decline.

Other scientists are more hopeful. They note that the number of grizzly mothers with cubs has edged upward throughout the 1980s in Yellowstone. In fact, the park's Interagency Grizzly Bear Study Team 1988 report found that this crucial number was the highest it has been since the dumps were closed. This is the best possible sign of grizzly recovery.

Frank and John Craighead have been busy with many projects since leaving Yellowstone. Going their own ways, they have continued to work to save the bear they know so well—Frank through the Environmental Research Institute, which he and colleagues established in 1955, and John through the Wildlife–Wildlands Institute, which he created in 1980. (Since 1986 it has been known as the Craighead Wildlife–Wildlands Institute.) In 1988 they were among fifteen world-famous scientists and explorers who received the National Geographic Society Centennial Award. The award honored them for a lifetime of scientific accomplishments.

Frank has always felt that scientists shouldn't write only for other scientists. So during the 1970s he wrote a nontechnical book about the study, *Track of the Grizzly*. In eloquent words it tells the story of Marian and her cubs, Beep and his brother, and all the Yellowstone bears who gave us the first-ever look at grizzly life.

Published in 1979, *Track of the Grizzly* has become a classic in its field. It is widely regarded as essential reading for all who care about the fate of grizzlies and America's national parks. Frank has au-

KAREN CRAIGHEAD HAYNAM

*John Craighead with a satellite map of
the Scapegoat Wilderness Area in Montana*

thored other books and continues to research, write about, and photograph wildlife. He has repeatedly visited Alaska to study the still-thriving grizzly population there.

John also wrote a book on the study; his is aimed at fellow scientists. Since he retired from the University of Montana in 1980, his base of operations has been the Craighead Wildlife–Wildlands Institute.

This institute is housed in rustic old log buildings on the outskirts of Missoula, Montana. Inside are offices for biologists working on field projects about caribou, Canada geese, and Rocky Mountain bighorn sheep. Outside, golden eagles are bred in captivity. Their offspring are released into the wild and tracked by radio and satellite. And here both John and his son Derek, who runs the institute, continue to study the grizzly.

One of John's most interesting projects takes up where "Operation Grizzly Bear" left off. He is using satellites to track grizzlies and to produce computerized maps of their environment. Companies that wish to build roads, cut timber, or drill for oil can use these maps to steer clear of areas most vital to grizzly survival.

Satellite maps have been made for parts of Montana, but Alaska is the main focus for this project because it is being developed so quickly. Frank's son Lance, and John's daughter, Karen, joined John and Derek on the initial work.

John's conservation work reaches around the

world. Since his summer in India as a young man, he has always been interested in Asia and Asian wildlife, and he was delighted to have the chance to visit Nepal in 1983. People there thought they had seen a new species of bear, and the king of the country invited John and other experts to see if they were right.

"The terrain in the Himalaya Mountains is rough, but King Birendra lent us his helicopter and pilot to get around," John recalls. "Unfortunately there was no new kind of Asian brown bear—just the young ones that can climb trees and the adults that are too heavy to climb."

But many good things came out of the visit. In 1986, King Birendra preserved for all time the "heart of the Himalayas" by joining it to Mount Everest National Park. China has since added its neighboring land. John and Derek have returned to Asia to advise local scientists. And when Asian officials came to America to tour our national parks in 1987, John led them through Grand Teton and Yellowstone. Like all visitors, they especially wanted to see some bears— but they did not.

What good is a grizzly? That question was posed by a rancher in a 1976 film by the Montana Department of Fish and Game. He didn't see the point of keeping wild lands wild. In his view, grizzly habitat was better used for livestock grazing and timber cutting.

As John Craighead sees it, there is a place for those

activities—but not in grizzly country. "By saving the grizzly, we save the land," he says. When an area is wild enough to support a grizzly, it is also home to about 250 other animal species and a wide variety of plant life. Opening grizzly habitat to commercial uses doesn't just force out the bears. It can destroy an array of wildlife and eventually erode the land itself.

What good is a grizzly? In 1960, Frank and John asked the question themselves in their first *National Geographic* article on the study. Almost thirty years later, their answers haven't changed.

"If we can't preserve the grizzly bear, we probably can't preserve ourselves," John replies. "The kind of behavior that allows the grizzly to become extinct is the same behavior that can destroy *us*. We know what the bear needs. The question is if we, as a society, can provide it."

Frank states, "If we lose the grizzly, the world won't end. But when you add up the losses, that's another story. If we lose the grizzly, the gray wolf, the bald eagle, the peregrine falcon—what will be next? We have to draw the line somewhere. Saving the grizzly shows that we *can* learn to save the rest of life on earth."

What good is a grizzly? Good enough to fight for, in the opinion of fifty-five thousand young people in Montana.

In 1982, Montana's secretary of state asked students in each public school to vote for the official state animal. The choice came down to grizzly bear versus

Students gathered in Montana's State Capitol to champion their choice of the grizzly bear as the official state animal.

WIDE WORLD PHOTOS

elk. The grizzly won in a landslide.

Some lawmakers were upset. They refused to sponsor the students' choice. "Several of my real close friends in the wood products and the sheep industry don't really idolize the grizzly," said State Senator Allen Kolstad. "Accommodations for grizzly bear habitat have really restricted options for the timber industry," said Montana Congresswoman Aubyn Curtiss.

The students didn't give up. Instead, five hundred of them jammed the State Capitol in Helena to fight for their choice. They carried posters and signs into the senate chamber: *Don't Be Square, Vote for the Bear. Get the Bear Facts. Bear Your Complete Thoughts. Vote Bear!*

For ninety minutes, one student after another stepped forward to testify. They championed the bear as "strong, courageous, independent, lovable, magnificent, wild, untamed, mighty, intelligent, brave, proud, adventurous, and fiercely unpredictable," according to a newspaper report in the *Missoulian*.

The students also urged the politicians not to tamper with democracy. They'd been asked to vote, and they expected their vote to count—even if some people disagreed with the outcome.

To the sound of wild cheering, the Senate Fish and Game Committee nominated *Ursus arctos horribilis* as Montana's state animal. Following a ninety-five to four vote in the State House, Governor Ted Schwinden signed the bill into law on April 7, 1983. It was another hard-won victory for the bear.

The grizzly bear is many things: a symbol of wildness, a source of national pride, a giant in the natural world—and in the human imagination.

Most people will never see a grizzly. But when Frank Craighead and John Craighead put a radio collar on a small female grizzly known as Number 40, they began to show the world how grizzlies live and die. It is up to us now to use the Craigheads' findings wisely, so that the grizzly bear can continue to roam free in the wild places of the earth.

BIBLIOGRAPHY

ADERHOLD, MIKE. "The Grizzly Bear: The Animal, the Symbol, the Enigma." *Montana Outdoors,* May/June 1982: 3–7.

———. "Montana's Rare Ones." *Montana Outdoors,* March/April 1988.

ASSOCIATED PRESS. "National Parks Urged to Ban All Concessions." The *New York Times,* May 26, 1988: 29.

BROWN, GARY. "The Yellowstone Perspective: Where Have All the Yellowstone Bears Gone?" *Western Wildlands,* Winter 1982: 28–30.

CAREY, ALAN. *In the Path of the Grizzly.* Flagstaff, Ariz.: Northland Press, 1986.

CHADWICK, DOUGLAS H. "Grizz—of Men and the Great Bear." *National Geographic* 144 (February 1986): 182–213.

CHASE, ALSTON. "The Last Bears of Yellowstone." The *Atlantic* 251 (February 1983): 63–73.

———. "The Grizzly and the Juggernaut." *Outside* XI (January 1986).

COLE, GLEN F. "Preservation and Management of Grizzly Bears in Yellowstone National Park." In *Bears—Their Biology and Management,* 274–288. Morges, Switzerland: International Union for Conservation of Nature and Natural Resources, 1970.

CRAIGHEAD, FRANK C., JR. *Track of the Grizzly.* San Francisco: Sierra Club Books, 1979.

———. "We Don't Bring 'em Back Alive." *Saturday Evening Post* 213 (October 12, 1940): 22–23.

CRAIGHEAD, FRANK C., JR., and JOHN J. CRAIGHEAD. "Adventures with Birds of Prey." *National Geographic* 72 (July 1937): 109–134.

———. "In Quest of the Golden Eagle." *National Geographic* 77 (May 1940): 692–710.

———. "Life with an Indian Prince." *National Geographic* 81 (February 1942): 235–272.

———. "We Survive on a Pacific Atoll." *National Geographic* 93 (January 1948): 73–94.

———. "Wildlife Adventuring in Jackson Hole." *National Geographic* 109 (January 1956): 1–35.

———. "Knocking Out Grizzly Bears for Their Own Good." *National Geographic* 118 (August 1960): 276–291.

———. "Trailing Yellowstone's Grizzlies by Radio." *National Geographic* 130 (August 1966): 252–267.

———. "Grizzly Bear Prehibernation and Denning Activities as Determined by Radiotracking." 1972. Wildlife Monograph No. 32. Publication of the Wildlife Society.

———. "Studying Wildlife by Satellite." *National Geographic* 143 (January 1973): 120–123.

———. "Tuning in on the Grizzly." In *Science Year 1973: The World Book Science Annual.* Chicago: Field Enterprises Educational Corp., 1973.

CRAIGHEAD, JOHN J. "Studying Grizzly Habitat by Satellite." *National Geographic* 150 (July 1976): 148–158.

CRAIGHEAD, JOHN J., J. S. SUMNER, and G. B. SCAGGS. *A Definitive System for Analysis of Grizzly Bear Habitat and Other Wilderness Resources.* Missoula, Mont.:Wildlife–Wildlands Institute, University of Montana, 1982.

CRAIGHEAD, KAREN. *Large Mammals of Yellowstone and Grand Teton National Parks.* Self-published, 1978.

CRAIGHEAD, KAREN, and DEREK CRAIGHEAD. "A Walk Through the Wilderness: Yellowstone at 100." *National Geographic* 143 (May 1972): 120–123.

CRAIGHEAD WILDLIFE–WILDLANDS INSTITUTE. Missoula, Mont.: *Annual Report,* 1987.

FROME, MICHAEL. "Are Biologists Afraid to Speak Out?" *Defenders,* July/August 1984: 40–41.

GEORGE, JEAN CRAIGHEAD. *My Side of the Mountain.* New York: E. P. Dutton, 1959.

———. *The Summer of the Falcon.* New York: Thomas Y. Crowell, 1962.

———. "The Day the Bears Go to Bed." *Reader's Digest* 89 (October 1966): 137–141.

———. "New Eyes and Ears on Nature." *National Wildlife* 10 (October/November 1972): 42–46.

———. *Journey Inward.* New York: E. P. Dutton, 1982.

"The Grand Illusion." *Newsweek* CVIII (July 28, 1986): 48–54.

Great Bear Foundation. *Bear News,* 1983–1988.

HORNOCKER, MAURICE. Letter to the editor. The *Wildlifer* 195 (November/December 1982).

JESSEN, STEVE. "What Good Is a Grizzly?" *Forsyth (Montana) Independent,* February 19, 1976.

MCNAMEE, THOMAS. *The Grizzly Bear.* New York: Alfred A. Knopf, 1982, 1984.

―――. "Putting Nature First." *Orion Nature Quarterly* 5 (Autumn 1986): 4–15.

The *Missoulian.* "Legislators Don't Want Grizzly as State Animal." January 16, 1983: 3.

―――. "Kids' Testimony Wins Backing for Grizzly Bill." February 18, 1983: 1.

―――. "House Favors Grizzly." March 15, 1983: 1.

―――. "Schwinden Signs Bear Bill." April 8, 1983: 1.

NATIONAL ACADEMY OF SCIENCES, Division of Biological Sciences, Assembly of Life Sciences, National Research Council. "Report of Committee on the Yellowstone Grizzlies." Washington, D.C., 1974.

OLSEN, JACK. *Night of the Grizzlies.* New York: G. P. Putnam's Sons, 1969.

SCHNEIDER, BILL. "Will This Grizzly Attack?" *Montana Outdoors,* February/March 1977: 4–6.

SHOLLY, DAN R. (Chief Ranger, Yellowstone National Park). Letter to author, undated; postmarked May 3, 1989.

U.S. Department of the Interior, Fish and Wildlife Service. *Grizzly Bear Recovery Plan.* 1982.

"What Good Is a Grizzly?" *Montana Outdoors,* July/August 1976: 13–14.

BOOKS FOR FURTHER READING

ANNIXTER, JANE AND PAUL. *The Year of the She-grizzly.* New York: Coward, McCann & Geoghegan, 1978.

CAREY, ALAN. *In the Path of the Grizzly.* Flagstaff, Ariz.: Northland Press, 1986.

DIXON, PAIGE. *The Young Grizzly.* New York: Atheneum Publishers, 1974.

GRAHAM, ADA, and FRANK GRAHAM. *Bears in the Wild.* New York: Delacorte Press, 1981.

HOSHINO, MICHIO. *The Grizzly.* San Francisco: Chronicle Books, 1987.

LAMPTON, CHRISTOPHER. *Endangered Species.* New York: Franklin Watts, 1988.

McCLUNG, ROBERT M. *Samson, Last of the California Grizzlies.* New York: William Morrow & Co., 1973.

———. *The True Adventures of Grizzly Adams.* New York: William Morrow & Co., 1985.

MILOTTE, ALFRED G., and ELMA MILOTTE. *Toklat: The Story of an Alaskan Grizzly Bear.* Edmonds, Wash.: Alaska Northwest Publishing Co., 1987.

PATENT, DOROTHY HINSHAW. *Bears of the Wild.* New York: Holiday House, 1980.

———. *The Way of the Grizzly.* New York: Clarion-Houghton Mifflin Co., 1987.

RADLAUER, RUTH S., *Yellowstone National Park.* Chicago: Children's Press, 1975.

SCHNEIDER, BILL. *Where the Grizzly Walks.* Missoula, Mont.: Mountain Press Publishing Co., 1977.

SETON, ERNEST THOMPSON. *The Biography of a Grizzly.* New York: Schocken Books, 1967.

TAWNEY, ROBIN. *Young People's Guide to Yellowstone National Park.* Stevensville, Mont.: Stoneydale Press, 1985.

WHITTAKER, BIBBY. *A Closer Look at Bears and Pandas.* New York: Franklin Watts, 1986.

INDEX